LIFE IN THE PUEBLOS

LIFE IN THE PUEBLOS

RUTH UNDERHILL

Ancient City Press
Santa Fe, New Mexico

Originally published in 1946 by the Bureau of Indian Affairs as *Workaday Life of the Pueblos.*

First Ancient City Press Edition

International Standard Book Number: 0-941270-68-8

Library of Congress Catalog Number: 90-085644

Edited and designed by Mary Powell

Cover art: Untitled painting, by Vidal Casiquito of Jemez Pueblo.
Blair Clark photographer, 1991. Courtesy of the Museum of Indian Arts and Culture/ Laboratory of Anthropology, Santa Fe, New Mexico, negative number 24037/13.

Library of Congress Cataloging-in-Publication Data

Underhill, Ruth Murray, 1883-1984
    Life in the Pueblos / by Ruth Underhill. — 1st Ancient City Press ed.
      p.   cm.
    Rev. ed of: Work a day life of the Pueblos, 1946.
    Summary: Introduces the daily life of the Pueblo Indians, past and present, describing their food, shelter, clothing, games, and other aspects of their existence.
    ISBN 0-941270-68-8 (pbk.)
    1. Pueblo Indians — Social life and customs. 2. Southwest, New — Social life and customs. [1. Pueblo Indians — Social life and customs. 2. Indians of North America — Southwest, New — Social life and customs.] I. Underhill, Ruth Murray, 1883-1984
    Work a day life of the Pueblos. II. Title.
    E99.P9U314   1991
    979'.00497 — dc20   90-85644
                                                                      CIP
                                                                      AC

CONTENTS

EDITOR'S FOREWORD

Anthropologist Ruth Underhill's popular study of family and village life of the Pueblo Indians was originally published by the Bureau of Indian Affairs as *Workaday Life of the Pueblos*. When published in 1946 it was a groundbreaking book on Pueblo lifeways that has become a popular classic for its depth and range in the study of everyday Pueblo life. In an effort to bridge the gap of time in the use of language, editing changes have been made in the area of ethnicity, gender, and anthropological references. While a major portion of the book has been left unchanged, the editors have edited the text so that the content of the book will remain enjoyable without any of the hindrances of out-dated terminology. In addition to these editing changes a couple of paragraphs have been added at the end to update changes in Pueblo life since 1946. Every effort has been made to remain true to the spirit and meaning of the original document while at the same time removing any barriers that the reader might otherwise have had.

It is our hope that a new generation of young and old readers can enjoy Ruth Underhill's classic work on Pueblo life and further develop an appreciation of the diversity of life that surrounds us.

PUEBLO PEOPLE

The great kiva at Pueblo Rinconada, Chaco Canyon, New Mexico

LONG BEFORE COLUMBUS ARRIVED, there were cities in the country now called the United States. They were built of stone or of dried earth almost as hard as brick. Their buildings rose three, four and even five stories high and might contain as many as a hundred or more rooms. Sometimes a whole town was actually one great apartment house, with space for a thousand people. Such towns were built in only one part of the country, the sunny southwestern plateau which now contains parts of five States: Arizona, New Mexico, Utah, Nevada and Colorado (see map page 3). Traveling through those states now, you may see the ruins of many of the ancient cities, but in Arizona and New Mexico, some twenty-eight of them are still inhabited by the people who first built them, the Pueblo Indians.

Pueblo is not the name of a tribe. It is the Spanish word for village and it was given by the Spaniards, coming up from Mexico. They found the Pueblo people living in their stone or earthen towns and also they found Indians who had no villages at all, but carried their dwellings with them in the shape of skin tents. They called the villagers Pueblo Indians by contrast. The Spaniards themselves did not know how great this contrast was, for, except for the pueblos of the Southwest, and a few other villages in southern Arizona, there were no other towns of stone or earth north of what is now the Mexican border. If the Spaniards could have explored all the present United States, they would have seen only villages of wood, or of wood and earth, and they could have gone a thousand miles to the north without finding villages at all. Most of the country, four hundred years ago, was occupied by people who lived in shelters of skin or bark or branches and who wore clothes of skin or wood fibre.

The Pueblo people had been living in the same general area for five hundred years and more. They did not need to wander in search of food, for they were growing corn, beans and squash. Nor did they need to wear skins, for they grew cotton or traded for it and wove it into clothing. They were making pottery which is considered a work of art to this day. They had an established government and a religion, with numerous officials and with regular ceremonies.

We have spoken of "Pueblo People" as though they were all one group and many people think of them as such. There is justification for this, for many of their customs are the same, in houses, clothing, crafts, even in ceremonies. Most important of all, they grew the same crops and this was the reason that they *were* pueblo or village people, rather than wandering hunters.

On closer view, however, they are not one group at all. They speak four distinct languages, with many dialects. Their pots and baskets are different for each village. So is their costume, if you know them well. Their government and ceremonies are different and each of the four language groups would have to be described separately. These pages do not take up that complicated side of their life, but even in describing the workaday activities we shall be constantly showing differences between one pueblo and another, or, at least between those of the River and Desert.

Pages 9 and 10 give a list of the language families to which pueblo people belong. A "language family" is a group of languages which have so much in common that linguists believe they must all have developed from one original tongue. That does not mean that the people who speak them can understand each other now, any more than Frenchmen, Germans and Spaniards, who also belong to the same language family, can understand one another. It may mean, however, that their ancestors lived together and shared many customs. When we know the language of an Indian group, we have a clue to its history. It is a faint clue, for linguists are still working out the language families and even groups of families.

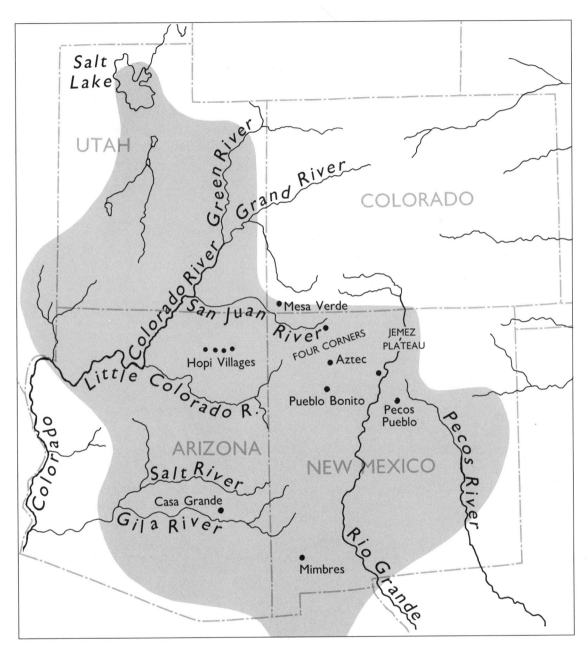

Map showing the area of the ancient pueblos.

We shall note their conclusions about Pueblo people as we name the different groups of villages and we shall have to admit that there is still much to learn.

To make some of these differences clear, turn to the maps on pages 3-7. The first shows the historic extent of Pueblo culture. Over much of the area few pueblos remain. Once there was more water than at present and once there were many more pueblos. Now in Arizona there remain only the Hopi. We take them up first, however, because this is the old territory of the pueblos and those who live in more fertile country arrived there long after the Hopi were well established.

The next map below shows the wavy outlines of three Hopi "Mesas"

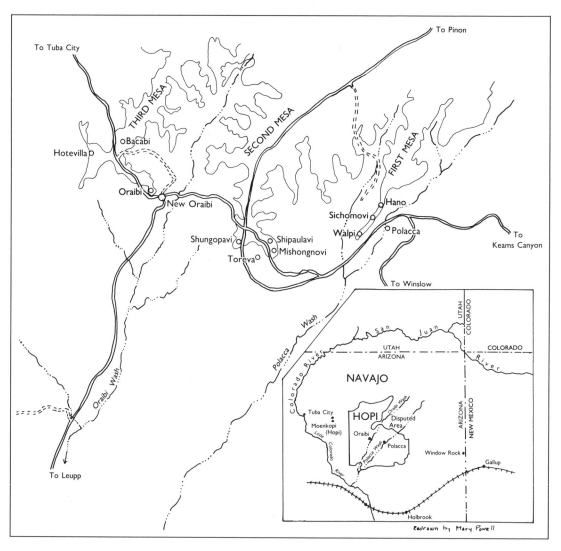

Map of the Hopi villages.

or flat topped, rocky heights, jutting out into the desert from the highlands of Colorado, like promontories into a sea. Mesa is the Spanish word for table and it is a good description of these low plateaus with the steep sides. There is no river near them. Still, all around the bases of the cliffs there are springs which rise underground far to the north and which flow in the driest weather. They, with the summer thunderstorms, supply the water for the crops.

There are eight or nine villages on these mesas, depending on how you count them. One, old Oraibi, has been inhabited continuously for a longer time than any other town in the United States. Around the mesas, on the flat land, are many ruins and the Hopi remember how they lived in some of them, before the Spaniards came and made them decide to move as far away as possible.

The language list shows that the Hopi belong to a huge language family known as the Uto-Aztecan. Its members stretch along the western uplands of America and include the Utes of Colorado and the Aztecs of Mexico. Speakers of Uto-Aztecan languages already described are the Paiute of the Great Basin, the Pima of the Gila River, their desert neighbors the Papago, and some of the "Mission" Indians of California. The Hopi have many points in common with all these people, both in their language and in some of their oldest customs.

Even the Hopi language is not always uniform, for people on the three mesas pronounce differently, and sometimes even use different words. Still, they understand each other, laughing at the differences as Easterners and Westerners laugh at each other. There is one Hopi town however which speaks quite differently. This is Hano, on First Mesa, occupied by a Tewa group, from the Rio Grande. Legend says that the Hopi gave them land on condition that they would help in fighting off enemies. Their village stands at the head of the trail, just where the enemy would arrive in the days when the mesa was climbed on foot.

Moving eastward along the desert, just as pueblo migration moved in ancient days, we come to Zuni, just over the border of New Mexico. This, too, is an old settlement, hidden behind a row of hills, beside a tiny river which may go dry in summer. Once there were six or seven pueblos here and the Spaniards told marvelous stories about them as the Seven Cities of Cibola. Now there is one large village with some summer camps. The Zuni language is so unlike the other Pueblo languages that it puzzled linguists for years. Now it, too, seems distantly connected with Uto-Aztecan. The connection is so slight however that the Zuni people must have been a long way from all the others who spoke languages of the same "family."

Zuni and Hopi have always journeyed back and forth on neighborly visits. They may have learned a great deal from one another, for they

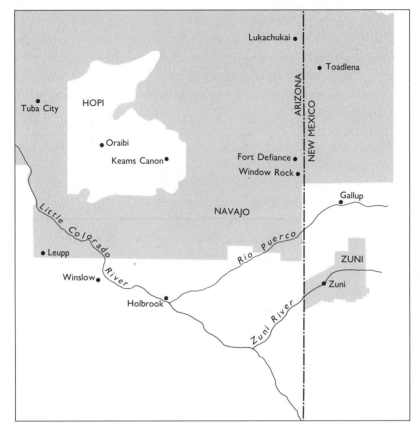

Map of the modern pueblos of Hopi and Zuni.

have many of the same customs. Much of their equipment was alike. They both got the same sandstone for houses and used the same devices in dry farming. They were far from the pueblos in the fertile valley of the Rio Grande that we shall speak of later. Often, we shall have to separate the two groups, speaking of Hopi and Zuni, with sometimes a neighbor or two, as the Desert pueblos. Others, with different materials and different contacts, we name the River pueblos.

Two pueblos (and in these days they have many extra camps and settlements) stand between River and Desert. These are Acoma (A'coma) and Laguna. Acoma, another ancient town, stands on a lofty mesa from which it flung the invading Spaniards down more than two centuries ago. It is a Desert pueblo in most senses, with houses built of stone, and with pottery like that of old Zuni. Its ceremonies are different, however, and much of its government is different. And it speaks the language of villages in the Rio Grande valley. This Keresan language is a linguistic orphan. No one is quite sure which family it belongs to and it will take a com-

Map of the modern Keresan and Tanoan Pueblos.

parison of its grammar and sounds before the scholars can say.

Laguna, the other midway pueblo, is also Keresan. But Laguna is what might be called a new settlement, made in Spanish days by refugees from Santo Domingo and Cochiti. Zuni, Acoma and even Navajo people have married into Laguna, so it is no wonder that it differs from the ancient towns to the west. Laguna is the Spanish word for lake and this town has always had a reservoir in addition to the tiny streams which help irrigate its broad fields.

Now we come to the River pueblos. Down the eastern part of New Mexico from north to south, there flows the Rio Grande (Great River), as the Spaniards named it. Its fertile valley was thick with pueblos in the old days and many of them are there still. Several little streams make their way to it, down rocky valleys, and one of these, Jemez Creek, still waters the fields of three pueblos. The villages of this watershed country differ, of course, in many ways. Still, they were alike in having water for their fields, which made them rich in contrast to the Desert pueblos. Many of them were not near rocky country, so they built their houses with earth instead of stone. They *were* near the wide eastern plains where the buffalo used to wander. They went there sometimes to hunt and to trade with the skin-clad Indians from east and north, who also hunted buffalo. No wonder their customs are often strikingly different from those of the desert.

Among them are Keresan Pueblos, related to Acoma and Laguna. On the map, you will note Zia and Santa Ana, on Jemez (Hay-mess) Creek, then Cochiti, Santo Domingo and San Felipe on the Rio Grande itself. Ruins on the rocky heights near these villages show that they were not always in the valley and they themselves remember how they camped on nearby mesas for years at a time, when they were fighting the Spaniards.

All other pueblos found today belong to a complicated language group, the Tanoan. It is not actually a member of the Uto-Aztecan family but perhaps distantly related. It is related, too, to a language of the buffalo plains, the Kiowa. Perhaps this indicates meeting and marriage between ancient Uto-Aztecans and ancient Kiowans. Did buffalo hunters move in from the Plains or did Pueblo people move out, long ago, to buffalo country? That page of old Southwestern history is still to be read.

Tanoan has three dialects, not intelligible to one another. Towa, the first, is represented by only one village, the prosperous Jemez, on the green plateau near the source of Jemez Creek. Pecos, further west, was inhabited until Spanish days but it was too near the Comanche. Its forty inhabitants gave up in 1840 and came to live at Jemez.

Tewa (Tay-wa) is a much larger division. Its villages have some of the best land of all, or they had, before the conquest. When there was famine in the Hopi desert, the Hopi came in droves to live with the Tewa and share their crops. It is a wonder that one group of Tewa ever cared to migrate to the barren Arizona mesas. Tradition is not certain just why the Hano moved but they have ties with their relatives on the Rio Grande even yet.

The Tiwa (Tee-wa) were once the largest division of all. Now they have only four villages but two of these, Taos and Isleta, are still large and prosperous. They are at the two ends of Tiwa country, Taos, far to the north, where the Rio Grande is narrow and tiny mountain streams flow into it; Isleta at the south in the wide fertile plains near Albuquerque. Once there were many further south and many between. Now, the southern ones have gone, and in between lies only little Sandia. She is hardly to be pitied, though, with her rich fields along the Great River. Up in the hills near Taos, perches one more tiny Tiwa town, Picuris (Pee-cu-rees) (See page 18 for old pueblos).

LIST OF PUEBLOS WITH THEIR LANGUAGE GROUPS

UTO-AZTECAN
    Hopi (First Mesa)
        Walpi
        Sichomovi
        Hano (Tewa language)
        Polacca
    Second Mesa
        Mishongnovi
        Shipaulovi
        Shungopovi
        Toreva (recent settlement)
    Third Mesa
        Oraibi
        New Oraibi (Kyakotsmovi)
        Hotevilla (recent settlement)
        Bacabi (recent settlement)

KERESAN
    Acoma
    Laguna
    Zia
    Santa Ana
    San Felipe
    Santo Domingo
    Cochiti

TANOAN (Aztecan-Tanoan, a proposed larger family than Uto-Aztecan,
        taking in very distant connections.)
    Towa
        Jemez (and descendants of old Pecos)
    Tewa
        Tesuque
        Pojoaque
        Nambe
        Santa Clara
        San Ildefonso
        San Juan
    Tiwa
        Taos
        Picuris
        Sandia
        Isleta

ZUNIAN (Probably related to Ute Aztecan)
    Zuni

The Eagle Dance at Cochiti Pueblo. Painting by Tonita Pena.

WHERE DID THEY COME FROM?

The throwing stick as used by the ancient Basketmakers

How did these various groups of people come together in the Southwest, settle down to farming and grow so much alike that they look, at first sight, like one tribe? Most of them say that they came from underground or else out of a lake. All agree that they wandered for a long time, dressed in skins and bark and eating wild seeds. Then, by a miracle, they learned about corn. Some groups tell how they met the beautiful Corn Maidens themselves, whose flesh is the corn of different colors. Some met the god of seeds, or perhaps only another tribe with greater knowledge. This is all that the poetic stories have passed on to us about the beginnings of farming, one of the greatest events in American history.

We know, however, that corn must have been raised in the Southwest some fifteen hundred years ago. That much we can tell from the earth itself, for, all through pueblo country, there are ruins of old houses, old rubbish heaps, old pits where corn was stored. Archeologists have been digging into such ruins for years, noticing every scrap of pottery and bit of string that they bring up and comparing it with other finds. Little by little they are working out a history of the Southwest.

This takes trained people, for they must know all about the history of the earth and about each animal bone or scrap of wood that they find. Such things can tell as much as a page of written history and to dig past them, looking only for a pretty pot, is like destroying such a page before it is read. The government realizes how important it is to keep these ruins from careless pot hunters and some of the larger ones are now national property. There are hundreds of smaller ones, however, and all who are interested in American history, regardless of their cultural background, can help to guard them for the future. This ancient book of the earth should be saved for careful reading, not left free to anyone who wants to dig up a pot to sell.

In the Southwest, a great deal of such reading has already been done, though some important pages of the book are still missing. We do not know where the Pueblo people came from, or when. The archeologists, however, can take us back at least two thousand years. At that time, they say, there were people in this broad area living on wild seeds. For hundreds of years these early Indians roamed over parts of Arizona, New Mexico, Nevada, Utah and Colorado. They dressed in breechcloths, skirts and sandals made from strips of yucca, a long-leaved desert plant. They

Baskets of the ancient Basketmakers.

made baskets and bags, instead of pots and boxes. They did not even have bows and arrows but hunted animals with a spear, thrown from a wooden handle. This throwing spear is called by its Aztec name, atlatl, and the picture on page 11 shows how it was used. The Indians who hunted with it must have lived under shelters of boughs, put up wherever they happened to be, for no houses are found.

Little by little archeologists can trace the change in these people. They find them learning to grow corn and squash, then beans. The earth does not tell us where this knowledge came from, any more than the Indian stories do, but it is thought that this knowledge traveled north, from countries with long histories, like Mexico and Peru. They find them learning to make pots, though whether they worked out the knowledge themselves or got it from others, the earth cannot reveal. They find them building a house of poles placed over a pit, a common kind of house in this desert country.

New people arrived, as archeological remains show. These sites show the long skulls of the old inhabitants, and side by side with them rounder skulls which must have belonged to a different people. These last are the dwellers in the pueblos today.

Ancient pueblo ruins at Pueblo Bonito, Chaco Canyon, New Mexico.

Ancient pueblo pots.

There is no sign of fighting. The new people must have arrived in small groups and lived peacefully with the old residents. Probably there were many inter-marriages. In fact, from this time on, we cannot tell which achievements belong to the newcomers and which to the old inhabitants. Scholars have decided to speak of them as one group and to call them by the Navajo name, Anasazi, Ancient People. Ruins show how the Anasazi began to use the bow and arrows, instead of the old throwing spear, how they raised cotton and finally, built stone houses. At first, these houses were separate, then several stood together and, at last, there rose the great apartment houses for which Pueblo people are famous.

We know about when this was, for nature has furnished a most interesting way of dating, by the trees. Trees grow from the center outward, by adding a new ring of wood each year. Each ring is different, depending on whether the season was wet or dry and in some kinds of trees, like pines, the difference is very plain. Scientists can slice through a pine tree, study its rings, and give a date to each one, beginning with the outermost, which must have been made the year the tree was cut. They can compare these rings with those in another tree, cut earlier, and so carry the dates back. Their tree calendar now reaches 11 A.D. They can use several kinds of trees, though not all, and they need not cut them down but only bore through to the center and take a sample slice. This can

Ruins of Cliff Palace at Mesa Verde, Colorado.

be done with the beams of old houses and therefore we know the dates of pueblo cities.

These were built about the year 1100 to 1300 A.D., a period late in the world's history. Already in the Old World the empires of Babylon, Egypt, Greece and Rome had come and gone. The modern countries of Italy, France and England were beginning to build their great cathedrals. The New World, however, was just coming into flower. The Incas, who built the most famous empire in South America, had only begun their rule. The Aztecs, famous conquerors in Mexico, were still on their migrations and did not even settle down until the great pueblo period was half over. Only the Mayas, oldest civilization of the New World, had already built two empires and were now giving way before other Indian peoples.

The great period of the pueblos lasted two hundred years. In that time, there were literally dozens of stone or clay towns built in the plateau country now called the Four Corners, where the states of Arizona, New Mexico, Colorado and Utah meet. Some were in river valleys, like Pueblo Bonito, Chettro Ketl, and Aztec in New Mexico, great single apartment houses, with their stories rising one behind another like giant steps. Some

The kiva at Ceremonial Cave, Bandelier National Monument, New Mexico.

were built high up out of the reach of enemies like Mesa Verde, Colorado, where the houses are crowded together under the roofs of open caves. Around all of them were fields of corn, beans and squash, and sometimes little reservoirs, terraces and ditches to hold the flood water. Inside the houses, men were weaving cotton garments and women were making beautiful pottery. In the open spaces before the villages were underground ceremonial rooms, like those of modern pueblos, and we infer that ceremonies were held there, just as they are held today.

Then something happened. One by one the great houses were deserted and no such magnificent ones were ever built again. Perhaps the reason was enemies and perhaps sickness. Yet more and more it looks as though the worst trouble was a change in the amount of rainfall. In those days the Four Corners, which is now nearly desert, had several streams and just enough rain that careful management would insure a crop every year. Then slowly the moisture grew less. The people in northern Arizona could no longer count on their crops. They left their houses in order, with no dead people, no signs of burning. It was a planned movement in which they slowly drifted east toward the Rio Grande. Colorado people, who moved later, had a drought of 24 years, so the tree rings show. No wonder they too moved down toward the green valley where there is always water.

This move had taken place before the first Europeans came. The Anasazi, who had once spread up into Utah and Nevada, were now almost all in New Mexico and, in fact, on the Rio Grande and its tributaries. A few stretched in a thin line across the middle of the State toward Zuni on the edge of Arizona, and Hopi, the only people who remained near the ancient country. But the Hopi had been lucky enough to find a place where springs seeped out at the edge of rocky cliffs, so they held on.

On page 18 is a map of the pueblo country as it was when the first Europeans first found it. They said seventy or eighty villages were here, although no one has been able to identify them all. Notice how far they spread down the Rio Grande — to Senacu, whereas now they stop just beyond Albuquerque. The Spaniards said they were dotted along both sides of the river for a hundred and fifty leagues, which is three hundred and seventy-five miles. Notice, too, how they stretch out past the mountains to the east where at present there are only ruins. All this country, from which the pueblos have now vanished, belonged to the Tanoans. Some of the towns were of the same subdivisions as Taos and Isleta (the Tiwa). One, Pecos, was Towa, like Jemez, and that held out longest of any of them. The other subdivisions, Tano and Piro, are completely gone.

The trouble was not rainfall this time. New, wild enemies, the Apache, had come from the north to rove the plains and these villages were too near their hunting grounds. During the seventeenth century those in the open country, the Tompiro, Tano and some Tiwa, were deserted one by one. They have been called "The Cities that Died of Fear."

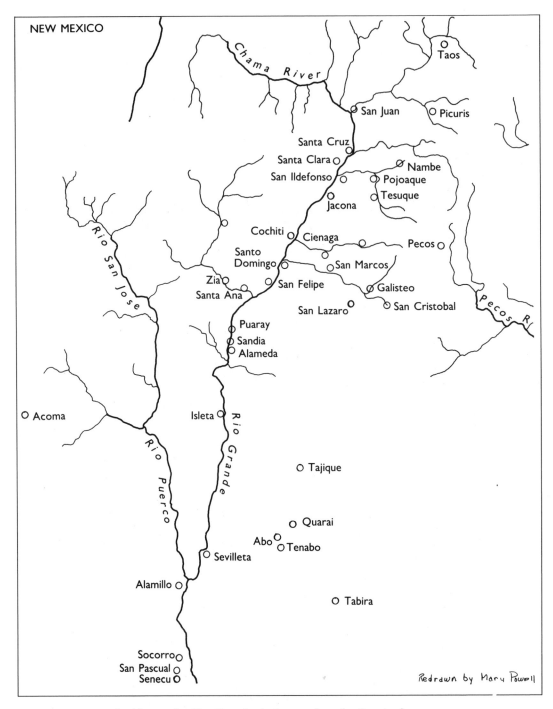

Pueblos in the Rio Grande drainage when the Spaniards came.

Coronado. Painting by Gerald Cassidy.

But there was an enemy more powerful than the Apache. In 1540, Coronado and his men, Spanish and Indian, rode up from New Spain, which was Mexico, to take possession of this unknown northern land. They stayed two years and detachments of them visited Zuni, Hopi and the Rio Grande. They reported that the country was poor, even though their expedition lived on corn they took from the pueblos, and wrapped themselves in pueblo cotton mantles. Coronado died, most of the horses died, some of the priests were killed and the rest of the party went back to Mexico. Little more happened until 1598.

That date, at the end of the sixteenth century, is the true beginning of Spanish rule in pueblo country. Then Don Juan de Onate came with colonists and their wives, with cattle and horses and sheep and settled down to stay. By that time Spain had worked out very strict rules about the way to treat conquered "savage" countries. The Indians, said the law, were not to be hurt or killed, nor was their land to be taken away. By that, the law meant the land they were actually living on. But there was a system by which the Spanish settlers could get a good deal from them, all the same. This was the system of encomienda, which means recommendation. The king of Spain, through his representative, the conquering leader, could give to each colonist a certain amount of land and could recommend to him the Indian villages on it. The colonist could not tear down the Indian villages nor build another within twelve miles of them, but he must teach them Christianity. To pay him for that, they must work for him and he would see that they were fed and clothed. In New Mexico they worked for the province under its governor.

This meant a great change in pueblo life. Of course it did not affect all the villages. Those in the western desert were so hard to reach that some of the Spanish governors never saw them. That is why Zuni and Hopi, to this day, retain so many of their old ways. But the pueblos on the Rio Grande were under the Spaniard's thumb. Some of the Tiwa tried to rebel, back in the days of Coronado, and had two villages burned and their people massacred. They did not try again. They all agreed to accept Christianity, though now and then a priest was killed in spite of that. When the Spanish colonists and the priests asked work from them, they gave it.

The Spanish brought with them new crops, animals and new ways of doing things. Many of these new ways were adopted by the pueblos. They began cultivating new vegetables, like wheat, chile and onions, new fruits like grapes and peaches. They learned better methods of irrigation, for one of the first things the Spanish did, with their iron tools, was to begin digging ditches from the Rio Grande. They learned how to use burros and horses. They got some sheep, as pay for their work, and soon they

A pueblo weaver using one of the very old style looms but with a heddle, or mechanism for separating the warp threads which was probably learned from the Spaniards.

began weaving with wool instead of cotton. They bought red cloth from the Spaniards, unravelled it, and so they had vivid red threads in their weaving for the first time. They had no vegetable dye that made very bright red. Pueblo people also learned to knit, since sometimes they were asked to knit hundreds of stockings for export to Mexico. They are knitting to the present day. We do not know whether they learned to embroider or only learned more about it. They may have been embroidering, just a little, with bone needles, for these are found in the caves of the Ancient People. They certainly learned much more about embroidery and got steel needles and new colors, though they kept their own designs.

There was one sharp break. It came in 1680, nearly a hundred years after the Spanish colonists had first settled down. In that year, the Indians felt they could not live under Spanish rule any longer and they organized the First American Revolution. It was the only time in their history that all the pueblos got together, but even then the union did not hold up for long. While it did, the people in the villages north of Santa Fe rose and killed every Spaniard they could find. Even the distant Hopi and Zuni joined. The Tewa laid siege to Santa Fe, where the Spaniards had their one fort, and it was not long before the governor and his men fled the pueblo country. They went to El Paso, which is now in Texas, and no Spaniards came back to stay for twelve years.

Those were a hard twelve years for the pueblos. Their crops failed. Their union fell apart. Some tried to make friends with the Spaniards. Some, like Cochiti, moved to the high mesas, where they stayed for many years after the rebellion was over. Navajo and Apache, with no Spanish soldiers to hold them back, spread over the country. Pueblo people lost their corn and their sheep. Whole Pueblo families gave up and went out to live with the wanderers. The Piro villages on the lower Rio Grande did not even try to hold out. They had not joined in the revolution because they had had some bad trouble with the Spaniards a few years before and had learned how useless such fighting was. When the Spaniards left, three of these Pueblos, Socorro, Servilleta and Alamillo, deserted their homes and went with them. They never came back but some of their survivors live to the present day in the Spanish-looking villages of Socorro, Texas, and Senecu, in Mexico.

The Spaniards, however, came back. After two or three trials a new man was appointed as governor and he found the pueblos ready to give up. De Vargas rode into Santa Fe at the end of summer, 1692, and that day is still celebrated. Every year descendants of the Spanish soldiers, dressed in brass helmets and leather coats, march into the Santa Fe plaza and stop before the governor's palace. Then the city dances for two days. The pueblos did not dance with joy, but they went on making pottery and tilling their fields while more and more settlers moved in, some taking Indian land. But there was no further widespread rebellion.

The next big change came when Mexico gained her independence from Spain in 1823. New Mexico, which was then only the northern part of old Mexico, was suddenly left without its old government and without any soldiers. The Navajo and Apache ran wild and all the colonists were too busy to think of Indian affairs. They were still too busy, when Mexico turned the country over to the United States in 1848 and Americans began to come in, trapping and trading. The governor of New Mexico was also supposed to be an Indian agent and he had his hands full with the Navajo and Apache. Often, he could not make the government at Washington understand that the peaceful pueblos were any different from these fighting Indians. In 1859 an Indian agent was appointed and finally a special one for the pueblos.

Ancient Basketmaker's coiled tray.

Their history since that time has changed as much or more than in all the 225 years they were under Spain. The reason was not so much the United States Government as the fact that railroads came through the country. Now at least, people could buy cheap dishes and cloth, glass for windows and furniture for houses. This was when many of the pueblos began to give up weaving and pottery making. Also they changed the old form of houses until now only Taos and Hopi, at the two ends of pueblo country, look much like the ancient villages.

We shall start our description of pueblo customs at this point. Generally we describe the ancient Indian ways as they were when the Europeans found them, but the Spaniards came to the pueblo country so long ago that it is hard to tell just what they did find. The old accounts are mixed and often they leave out the very things we want to know. So we shall describe the pueblos as they were found about 1880, noting the changes that must have come during Spanish rule.

CULTIVATED CROPS, STORAGE AND COOKERY

Hopi woman shelling corn

THE MAIN FOOD OF THE PUEBLOS was Indian corn. One writer thinks, in fact, that it must have formed eighty per cent of their diet. They were grateful to this permanent crop, which had allowed them to settle down among their fields, instead of wandering with the seasons. Zuni thought of it as the flesh of the magical Corn Maidens. The Keres believed in a Corn Mother, who sent all growing things and was the mother of people also. There was hardly a ceremony in which corn, or cornmeal, was not used. Pueblo people never made animal sacrifices (indeed, few American Indians did), but when they wished to ask favors of the supernatural Beings, they scattered cornmeal.

Corn was of many different kinds. People who are not farmers may speak of corn as though it were but one kind of plant, but farmers know better. They speak of flint corn, with its hard kernels that will keep for years;

flour corn, so easy to grind; and dent corn, with its dimpled kernels, the prime food for cattle. Pueblo people had all of these. They began fifteen hundred years ago, with flint with little yellow ears like those shown in the photograph above. Later they had dent and flour. They did not have sweet corn and popcorn, scholars speculate, until Europeans brought it to them from other Indians.

Through the years, before this happened, they were developing the corn they did have. By 700 A.D. they had several varieties and soon they had these in different colors. We who think of corn as being mostly yellow and white, would be amazed to see a string of pueblo ears, pink, black, blue and speckled. There are traditions of many-colored Indian corn from all over the country but we hear more of its importance in the pueblos than anywhere else. There were four main colors, named for the four directions from which the winds blow: yellow for north, blue for west, red for south, and white for east. Most of them also named black (really dark purple) for underground and many-colored for above. They were careful to keep the colors separate in planting, but naturally there were mixtures. A bunch of pueblo corn, hanging against a wall, has as many shadings as a bouquet of flowers.

No one farmer raised all the varieties. In some towns, like Hopi, where there were at least nineteen different sorts, seeds were the property of families, carefully guarded and never given away except when a young man married and went to live with his wife's people. Then he brought with him some of his own cherished kernels for the first planting of his wife's field. We can imagine that a boy whose family owned some specially good seed, was much sought as a bridegroom.

All the pueblos paid special attention to their seed corn, sometimes leaving prayer feathers with it as did the Zuni, or twigs of evergreen as did the Tewa, since the never-dying evergreen has a magic for growth. The dark inner rooms of pueblo houses were used for corn storage and each family often had a whole room where the ears were stacked like cord wood, each color separately. They tried to have enough for a year in advance, or even two, for there were seasons of drought when the whole crop might be lost. Those whose stores were used up would leave in troops to visit other pueblos. The Hopi, for example, went to the Rio Grande Tewa as late as 1864.

Drought was a constant danger. Those villages which had moved to the Rio Grande were fairly safe, for they had moist fields beside an ever-flowing stream and even before the Spaniards came they seemed to have dug a few simple ditches. Those on the tributary streams had more trouble, yet all needed rain as well as river water and they prayed for it earnestly. Villages in the desert, like Hopi, had no visible water and were lucky if they got a shower or two before August. Yet they solved their difficulty.

Corn drying on the roof tops, San Juan Pueblo, New Mexico.

Their methods of dry farming must have come down from the days of the great houses or even earlier and, considering the tools they had, they were the best possible.

The tools were pieces of wood. One was a tough stick, about four feet long, with one end sharpened and hardened in the fire. This was used for breaking up the ground and also for making deep holes to contain the seeds. In some pueblos, it was merely a straight stick and the farmer knelt to use it as he does in the drawing on page 33. In others, it had a broken off branch, which serves as a footrest, as shown on page 32. This was the spade. The hoe was a shorter and wider piece of wood, sometimes called the sword hoe, because it was flat like a sword and sharpened along one edge. A man knelt and scraped this along the ground, cutting off the tops of the weeds.

With such tools, there was no chance of turning over the earth deeply, as a farmer does with his plow. But, in pueblo country a plow would have been a mistake. If there was any moisture at all in the clay soil, it was deep underground, where the overflow from springs or the remains of a dried up stream, seeped through the earth a foot or more below the surface. The farmer had to leave the crusty cover of the ground untouched, to protect this moisture, and then plant his corn deep down so the roots would get to it. Half his problem was to find the spots where this could be done, and generations ago the villages had attended to that. Every family had fields of this kind scattered over the unpromising-looking desert, so that if one crop failed perhaps another would not.

The fields were planned to catch the summer rain, also. The farmers knew where the torrents from the hills would come rushing down in August and in the fan-shaped space between the hills where the earth had been washed down by these yearly floods, they placed their cornfields. Those fields would soon be washed away and filled with gullies if they did not control the water, so they built little dams of brush and earth to check it and make it spread. At Zuni, you can still see such dams, spreading out from the water channel like the veins of a leaf while the whole field has a wall of earth to hold in the precious water. The Hopi, who have stronger torrents to deal with, make dozens of little dams, sometimes around separate plants. All summer the farmers must be repairing their dams, filling up channels which have grown too deep, leveling off lumps of earth which the stream has brought down. Yet they say proudly that where the Pueblo farmers have been working, there are no deep gullies to ruin the land.

These fields in the path of the water courses may lie far out on the desert, so far that a man has to run ten miles, or ride his burro or, at Zuni, camp there for the summer. Every family, also, has a small choice plot or two, directly under the drip of a spring at Hopi or, at Zuni, beside the little river which has water underground, if not above. If the season is dry, Zuni women carry water out to their gardens in jars. Here they grow early corn and, in these days, modern vegetables like chile and onions. Every handful of the precious, moist earth is carefully tended and each plant stands in a little square compartment, surrounded with ridges of earth to hold in the water. "Waffle gardens" they are called in English, and the photograph on page 30 taken in Hopi country shows how like waffles the regular, criss-cross ridges really look.

Planting in these gardens began in early May. In the open fields it must wait until all danger of frost was over and for this, many villages had an official sun watcher. This man observed the sunrise every morning and when it took place exactly behind a certain gap in the hills he knew that warm weather had come to stay. Then the news was cried out to the village. Sometimes they planted first a field for the town chief who spent his time working for the village and often feeding people too. Then groups of relatives and neighbors would gather for their own planting, all working together on field after field.

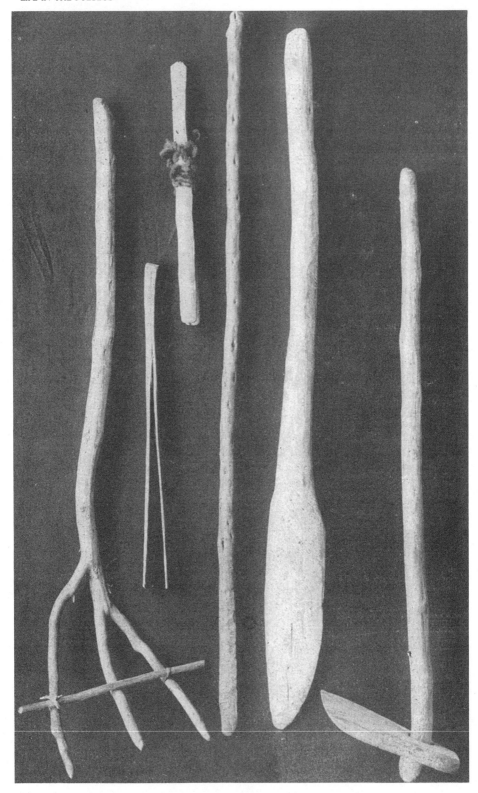

Ancient pueblo agricultural tools, Hopi Pueblo.

The fields were ready, for often the farmers had been out since February, mending the dams and building fences of brush against the fierce winds that sweep over the desert in the spring. They had not removed the old corn plants, however. Anglo farmers take in the corn stocks after Halloween and feed them to the cattle, but then, they plan to plow and fertilize next year. The Pueblo farmer, in his different situation, was just as practical. He had no fertilizer and he used the same fields each year — but not the same part of the fields. The new plants were always placed between the stalks of the old so that, while one part of the field was working, one was resting. That was possible with corn which, from the beginning, must have been planted by hand in holes, spaced far apart, not sown broadcast like wheat. The Indians taught the Europeans their spacing system which is followed to this day.

A Hopi garden, receiving water seepage from the cliffs.

Hopi "waffle gardens."

Walking between the old corn plants, the men sank their digging sticks deep — sometimes eighteen inches — so that the corn roots would get to moisture. Farmers from the moist eastern states can hardly believe this, for they are used to planting corn just below the surface and "hilling it up" as the eastern Indians taught them. But the Pueblo people knew what they were doing. Their corn was of the sort to make long roots and short, tough leaves able to withstand the winds of desert country. Twenty kernels or so were dropped into each hole, so that some would be sure to live. When they came up, they would not be tall stalks like the eastern corn, eight or ten feet high and "growing so fast you can't chop it in the same place twice." They would be low, spreading bushes, growing in a dense clump so that, even if the wind tore the outer ones to shreds, there would be protection for the ears at the center.

The corn of the pueblos, particularly the desert ones, Zuni and Hopi, is a real contribution to American agriculture. It will live through a drought that might kill other varieties. It has a short growing season which allows it to ripen between the last frost of spring and the first of fall on the high Southwestern plateau. And it is immune to many diseases that destroy other corn. Commercial farmers and even our own Department of Agriculture are considering the mixing of this ancient corn, in its numberless variations with some of the tenderer and more standardized strains. It may turn out a monument to Pueblo civilization quite as important as the ruined apartment houses.

We have told of the practical side of planting. Yet the Pueblo farmer felt that, in the risky task of growing food for the people, prayers and offerings were equally necessary. At Hopi and Zuni, men went racing over the plain before planting time as they hoped the torrents would race down the water courses, kicking a stick or a ball of clay before them, as the stream would roll the debris. The Tewa played shinny with a buckskin ball, full of seeds, until it burst and scattered its contents over the earth. Those villages which had irrigation ditches opened them with prayer and ceremony, throwing feather offerings into the waters. When it was time to place the seeds in the earth, there was a ritual for each individual farmer. This is the prayer of an old time Laguna man:

> "Mother, Father, you who belong to the great Beings, you who belong to the Storm Clouds, you will help me. I am ready to put down yellow corn and also blue corn, and red corn and white corn and all kinds of corn. I am going to plant today. Therefore you will help me and you will make my work light. You will not make it heavy and also you will make the field not hard. You will make it soft."

Many rituals were even longer, like those described at Zuni fifty years ago. Some morning in May the Sun Watcher would be heard calling from the housetops that planting time had come. Then each farmer hurried to his corn room to get the special fawnskin bag in which he kept his seed corn. Zuni was one of the towns which had an especially elaborate treatment for seed corn and this had been prayed over and also sprinkled with a mixture of paint, salt, flowers, and flower pollen, all holy things. The cornfield had been prayed over, too. In the center the farmer had planted one of the pueblo messages to the gods, a stick decorated with the feathers of summer birds, which bring the rain. Now he took his planting stick and made six holes around the feather offering, in six directions: north, west, south, east, with northwest to represent *above* and southeast for *below*. He put four corn kernels of the appropriate color into each hole, singing:

> Off yonder toward the northland (or south, east, etc.)
> May it but prove that my yellow corn grains (or other color)
> Shall grow and bear fruit,
> Asking which I now sing.

Then he planted the rest of his corn in rows, radiating out from the center, each color by itself. This form of planting must be very old, for the Navajo learned it from the pueblos. The Hopi, however, now plant in parallel rows. They, too, make offerings, and smoke over the field. Women throw water on the men as they go out to plant, as a call to the rain to do as they are doing. Sometimes the masked figure of the

A Pueblo gardener using digging stick with footrest.
Drawing by Charles Loloma, Hopi.

god, Maasawu, who owns the soil, may appear by request and run around
the field.

The planting was often done by parties of relatives on both sides of
the family and by neighbors. The women spent the day cooking. These
were women of the family to which the field belonged, for land and houses
were usually female property in the pueblos. Their girls, dressed in their
best, brought lunch to the field and before sundown, a great supper was
ready for the workers.

When hoeing time came, parties worked in the same way. However,
weeds, in this dry country, were not such a bad problem as the hungry
birds. No one ever thought of more schemes to keep away the birds,

A Pueblo gardener, using digging stick without footrest.
Drawing by Charles Loloma, Hopi.

and especially crows, than the Zuni. They stretched strings on stakes across their fields, like a forest of clotheslines, and from the strings they hung rough scratchy cactus leaves. They arranged nooses of hair to catch the crows, and they caught plenty. They made scarecrows in every horrible shape. Children and old people stayed in the fields while the corn was ripening, shouting and throwing stones to scare the birds.

Meantime, the people in all the villages were praying and dancing for rain, and, if all the ceremonies were properly carried out, it came and the crops grew ripe. First came the early corn, planted in sheltered nooks and sometimes even watered by hand. The Hopi planned to have theirs ready for Niman, the midsummer festival. Then the juicy fresh food was handed out to the children as a surprise.

Hopi and Zuni both roasted this corn in outdoor pits in the cornfields. The pits were about ten or twelve feet deep and three feet across. They were filled half full of kindling which burned and died to ashes, then the corn ears were put in, still in their husks, then stones and then hot embers. This formed a sort of fireless cooker in which the corn was left from late afternoon to sunrise. The milky young corn tastes delicious and must have seemed especially so in days when it was the first fresh vegetable after months of dried food. Another treat at harvest time was kernels of this corn crushed lightly to a milky mass and made into a cake which was baked on a hot stone. Non-Indians who taste this today call it corn macaroon.

Then came the hard, colored corn from the fields. In every pueblo, this was a time of festival. The Tewa, of San Ildefonso, swept their whole village before the ripe ears were brought in and dumped before the houses. Corn, they said, was like a person and would not care to come in if the town was dirty. The Zuni farmer carried the first ears into the house as reverently as though they were the Corn Maidens themselves, and his wife and the other women welcomed them with a little ceremony.

"My children," said the wife, speaking in the regular phrase of greeting, "How be ye these many days?"

Answering for the corn, the other women gave the polite response: "Happily, happily."

Then the new ears were sprinkled with corn meal and laid in the store room.

Everywhere, families with their relatives gathered to do the husking, joking and flirting while they sorted the ears by colors. Tewa boys of the Rio Grande used to look for an ear with no kernels on it for they had a right to chase some girl with it, teasing her about how she hated to grind corn and was as useless as that "lazy grass." It might end by the girl being rolled in the corn stalks, shouting that no matter how lazy she was, she would never marry that good-for-nothing boy.

The best ears were laid aside for seed, some leaf and stem being left on them, so they could be braided and hung up. It is these bunches of colored seed corn which we so much enjoy for wall decoration. The other ears were spread out to dry until the roofs of the village seemed carpeted with them. No sight in pueblo country is more beautiful than the storied houses of Taos on the Sunday after harvest. Then every doorway is hung with strings of corn ears, bright as bunches of hollyhocks. The roofs groan under stacks of yellow, red, black and blue ears, each heaped together. In every yard, men and women are braiding, tying and stacking while the wagons lumber over to the church, piled with brilliant colored ears which will help pay the priest for his year's services.

Except at Taos, the men's connection with the corn ended when they brought the crop to the village. After that, it belonged to the women. It would be their task to sort it over during the winter, throw out mouldy ears and sometimes dry it again. After special ceremonies, there would be a sprig of evergreen or a prayer feather to be placed with it for extra luck as it was stacked away in the corn room. Often, some of it must be ground up with turquoise and white shell as an offering to the great Beings. The corn room was one of the most important parts of a pueblo house.

Besides corn, Pueblo people raised two kinds of squash (properly called pumpkin, the botanists say). These were the large green Cucurbita moschata and the smaller, striped Cucurbita pepo. When a pumpkin was brought in from the fields, the rind was hacked off with a stone knife or, later, a metal one. The fruit was cut in half and hung up in the sun for a few days. When the thready part in the center had dried out and the meat was soft, each half was cut round and round in a long spiral strip. This was dried thoroughly and then wadded up in a bundle to be kept. When soaked in water, its delicious pumpkin taste returned.

Then there were beans. It was the Indians of America who discovered and domesticated most of the beans we now know and Pueblo people had two kinds. One was the large kidney bean (Phaseolus vulgaris) grown by Indians all the way from Peru to New York and New Mexico. The other was the little-known bean called tepary (Phaseolus acutifolius, var. latifolius) grown only in Mexico and the Southwest. It is only recently that merchants have learned about this bean, whose remains can be found in ruins of the Anasazi. It grows wild in northern Mexico and in sheltered canyons of Arizona so it must have been Indians of those regions who first cultivated it. Here is one plant that did not come from Peru or the Aztec country. It was probably first raised by Indians a little further south than the Pueblo people, but at least the pueblos had it in many shades of red and white and spotted. Beans are a good source of protein, the same food element that we get in meat. Now that we are all growing so

A modern Jemez woman husking corn. Note the speckled and colored corn in foreground.

Pueblo women winnowing beans. Drawing by Velino Herrera, Zia.

careful of diet, it is interesting to know that the Pueblo people, who did not get much meat, had plenty of beans and made good use of them.

Beans of different colors were planted separately, to keep the strains pure. When they were harvested, men threshed them with sticks to break open the pods. Then women generally winnowed them in a basket tray, just as women once winnowed wild seeds. The tray was a flat one of coarse basketry which was shaken gently until the light pods and chaff came to the top. Then the woman gave it a quick tilt to let the breeze carry the trash away, leaving the heavier beans. The sketch above shows how this was done.

Beans and squash had a place in ceremonies, though not as great a one as corn. Artificial squash blossoms were placed on some of the altars to lend their growth magic. The Hopi held a February ceremony (Powamu) when they raised small bean plants in the warm underground ceremonial rooms, then paraded them through the village for good luck in the coming summer's planting.

One other crop raised in the pueblos, or at least by the Hopi, was sunflowers. They were not the huge ones grown by Anglos today nor even the smaller, wild ones that line the roads in some of our western states. They were a special variety which the Hopi must have domesticated long ago, for seeds are found in the ruins. Do not imagine that they were grown merely for beauty, though sunflower decorations had a place in many ceremonies. Many spectators at the Snake Dance have seen the ceremonial runners come back after dawn, bringing sunflowers and fresh cornstalks for the maidens to tussle over. The girl who gets one of them will have luck for the year. More practically, sunflower seeds are a good source of oil. People who had no butter, no olive oil and little fat, made good use of them. They roasted them, too, and ate them for pleasure as we eat peanuts.

These are the old-time crops but if you visited a modern pueblo, you would see plenty of newer ones. Wheat came in with the Spaniards, two hundred and fifty years ago, and so did the methods for its cultivation.

Jemez women cutting wheat with a sickle.

Threshing wheat with horses, Taos Pueblo.

In fact, if you wanted to picture a farm in old Spain, you could sometimes get a better idea of it in New Mexico than in Spain itself. Up to the beginning of this century the wheat was cut with a hand sickle. Then it was threshed in the old European manner, which goes back to Biblical times. This meant clearing a circular space on the ground, wetting it until it was hard and then fencing it in. This is the "threshing floor." When it was ready, the wheat was piled in the center, perhaps around a pole which would keep it in place. Men stood on top of the pile to pitchfork it down. Then some sheep, goats or horses were driven round and round until their hard hooves had trodden the grain out of the husks. Husks and grain had to be separated and this was done by a woman who tossed them up in a basket, just as she did the beans. The light husks flew off in the wind and the grain remained. Then she washed the grains, using a loose woven basket for a sieve, as Jemez women do still (See photograph on page 40).

Now and then, outside some pueblo, you may still see three or four horses prancing around in this way. But today you are more likely to hear the whir of a threshing machine and to find the farmers gathered to help with it. Beside wheat, you will see alfalfa, growing in irrigated fields watered

Washing the threshed wheat, Jemez Pueblo.

from government storage reservoirs. Then there will be yellow dent corn for the cattle and other field crops. The pueblos have learned new methods from American farmers, just as they learned about wheat from the Spaniards and about corn from other Indians.

There are new plants in the home gardens, too. The chile peppers, which hang in picturesque red strings outside so many houses, were brought from Mexico by the Spaniards, as were bell peppers, and later, tomatoes. Cabbage, lettuce, onions, peas, beets, radishes, came from Europe. So did watermelons and fruit trees. Isleta, on the Rio Grande, now has outstanding orchards and vineyards, with a good sale of fruit. Hopi, even in its desert country, has peach and apricot trees, planted over underground water. Most of them are raised from seed and anyone may plant a few where there is a good spot. Several families have large orchards and camp in them for a week in September, cutting the fruit in halves and spreading it to dry in the sun. The wrinkled brown halves look something like a human ear and "ears" is what they are called, in many Pueblo languages.

COOKING VEGETABLES

Corn, the principal food, was not easy to cook. There is no trouble when it is fresh, for then it can be boiled or roasted in a few minutes. Pueblo people had to keep it for years and eat it day after day. Their corn, as we have mentioned, was usually flint corn, which has hard kernels, needing hours of cooking to soften them. Pueblo women had several ways of doing this. One was to grind the kernels to flour before boiling; one was to roast them until the shell cracked. One was to soak them in something like lime or lye, which would melt the shell off. Pueblo people used mostly the grinding method. They had some thirty or forty ways to cook corn and all but a few required that the sun-dried kernels should first be ground into flour.

A Pueblo girl had to spend three or four hours a day grinding corn. Her flour mill consisted of three or sometimes four flat stones of different degrees of smoothness (page 78) and a small cylindrical stone which she rubbed up and down over them. When she needed flour, which was every day, she stripped the kernels from some ears of corn and laid them on the coarsest stone, then knelt behind it with the small stone in both hands and crushed them as fine as she could. The corn grew a little moist and sticky in the process, so she put it in a pot over the fire and toasted it crisp. Then she ground it on the next stone, and so on.

When she rose from the third or fourth stone her knees might be numb from kneeling. Nevertheless, every girl was expected to grind three or four quarts of meal a day, and a Hopi girl was not married until she had ground at her fiance's house for four days to show what she could do. Three or four girls sometimes did this together, one at each stone, and the Zuni and western Keres had a ceremony in which they ground corn to music. All finished their grinding at the same time and each passed on her basket of meal to the girl at the next finer stone, with motions as rhythmical as if she were dancing. Girls do not like to grind now, say the older women, because it is so hard on their hands. At least, they are asking to use the soft flour corn and the old women do not like that. Flour corn does not resist mold and rats as the old flint used to do.

Ground cornmeal could be made into many sorts of bread, dumplings or gruel, all with different names. Most important was bread, and particularly the wafer bread, for which the pueblos are famous. It is known by the Hopi name, *piki* (pee-kee).

For this, women had what we might call a stone stove, consisting of a specially smooth flat stone, which rested on four stone supports, so that a fire could be built under it. They mixed a batter of cornmeal which was spread lightly over the stone with the fingers laid flat. It was so thin that it cooked instantly and was peeled off again to be piled in a dish and later folded up. It took a girl years to learn the skill for this kind

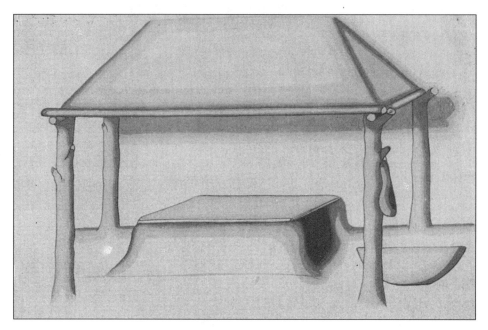

An oven for wafer bread, Hopi Pueblo.

of bread making. Some pueblos still make this bread, especially the Hopi and Zuni. They generally use blue cornmeal, but the blue turns gray in cooking so they mix in some ashes of salt bush, bean vines, juniper, sheep dung or, in these days, baking powder, to fix the color. The Hopi also make a pink or yellow wafer bread dyed with flowers which they raise for the purpose in their small irrigated gardens. The pink color comes from coxcomb (Amaranthus cruentus), and yellow from safflower (Carthamnus tinctorius).

Wafer bread was generally made in quantities once a week or so and kept. When it got stale, it could be broken up and the crumbs retoasted in a pot, to be fried in grease or soaked in water before eating. A thicker sort of bread was made by mixing coarsely ground meal with water and adding some water from slaked lime to give a greenish color. This was baked on the same sort of stone as the wafer bread but did not take so much skill. For a change, the women would make dumplings. These were lumps of cornmeal, blue, white, salted or unsalted, sweetened or unsweetened, made into a dough and dropped in a pot of boiling water. Sometimes, before boiling, a lump of dough was wrapped in a cornhusk and meat or flavoring was placed inside it. This was a favorite dish of Indians in the Southwest and Mexico. We know it by its Mexican Indian name, *tamale*.

Gruel was made of cornmeal dropped loose into boiling water. This was the regular morning drink before Pueblo people began to use coffee. The cornmeal might be blue or white and it was usually whipped while boiling to make it frothy. A kind of gruel used in traveling was famous all over the Southwest. This was *pinole*. It was made of corn roasted at harvest time, then later ground fine, with the usual toasting between each two grindings. This meal was already so well cooked that the traveler needed only to mix it with cold water to have a nourishing drink.

Pueblo people had no sugar until the Europeans came, but they had worked out a way to get at the sugar in corn. Today this is done by a chemical process which makes corn syrup, often substituted for maple. Pueblo people used a chemical process too — the action of chewing in a human mouth. Fine cornmeal was chewed and added to a batter of meal and water. The saliva brought out in chewing combined with the corn-starch to make sugar. Those selected to chew were young girls, whose mouths were clean, and before they performed their task they kept spurge root in their mouths for days, to sweeten their breath.

These recipes and some twenty more, all require grinding the corn. Another way to get rid of the shells was to soak the corn in wood ashes which make lye. After a time the shells fell off and the starchy inside of the kernel swelled to twice its natural size. Corn in this state is called hominy and was a great favorite of eastern Indians. Pueblo women sometimes made it too, and also they ground up the swollen kernels and made them into the corn pancakes which are known by their Mexican name, *tortilla*. These are now found all over the Southwest and Mexico.

Wheat bread was made in the old Spanish style, for Pueblo women learned about it at the same time their husbands learned to grow wheat. They also learned to make the beehive ovens (Spanish *horno*) described on pages 85-86. These contain only one chamber, not a firebox and bake-oven like a modern stove, and they cannot hold fire and bread at the same time. The woman makes a fire on the oven floor and lets it burn, tightly closed, for hours. When it has burned out, she sweeps the oven and puts in the bread. This was a regular fashion, two or three hundred years ago, and the pioneers in New England baked their beans on the same system, placing the pot in a little cupboard in the chimney wall. The bread, too, is mixed in the old style, used by all women when yeast was scarce. Instead of yeast, the woman uses the ferment in a little dough, kept from her last baking. She mixes this with flour and water and kneads it well. Then she shapes it into little round loaves, the size of a small pie.

Today, when packaged bread is bought at the stores, the beehive ovens still have plenty of use. On the day before a festival, half the women in a pueblo may be seen, first heating their ovens, then placing the loaves inside them with a long wooden shovel. On that important winter day

Baking bread in the beehive oven, San Ildefonso Pueblo.

at Zuni, when the clowns are paid for their year's work, files of ten or twelve women walk into the plaza, bearing on their heads trays covered with a cloth and loaded with these little wheaten loaves.

Pueblo women made a sweet food out of wheat also, not by chewing this time, but by sprinkling it with water and letting it stand in a warm place until it sprouted. The sprouted wheat was ground up, mixed with a batter of flour and water and baked all night between layers of hot stones. The result was something like sweet crackers.

Drying peppers and melons, Jemez Pueblo.

There were not so many ways for cooking the other vegetables as there were for wheat and corn. Squash could be roasted whole in the ashes and it was when it was fresh. Of course, too, it could be cut in pieces and boiled. The squash used in winter was that dried in bundles as shown above. To cook this, the woman broke up the bundle and boiled it. Squash seeds were saved, for they might be pounded to give oil for cooking. Also they could be toasted in a jar, cracked and eaten like sunflower seeds. Even squash flowers were sometimes fried, as a great delicacy.

Beans were usually boiled. After they were cold they could be made into wafer bread by pounding them to a paste and mixing with cornmeal batter. Usually they and other vegetables were cooked in a stew with corn or meat.

WILD CROPS AND HOW THEY WERE USED

Pine Nut

CORN, BEANS AND SQUASH WERE fresh once a year, at harvest time, but during the other eleven months or so the people had to eat them in dried form. Their only way of getting fresh vegetables was to seek for the wild roots, greens and berries which ripened at different times during the summer. Each pueblo used those which grew in its own neighborhood, probably many more than are given in our list. It would be interesting to have further information on this practical subject. Indians and researchers living in pueblo country could help greatly by special studies in different villages.

For those interested in such a study, the plants known are listed at the end of this chapter. Here, we give a summary which tells what a variety of things were used. It shows that the pueblos had equivalents for the nourishing roots such as potatoes and carrots; for greens, such as lettuce and spinach; even for delicacies, like celery or cress. They had quite as many flavorings as the modern woman keeps in cans on her kitchen shelf

Rocky mountain bee plant. Drawing by Charles Shirley, Navajo.

and they achieved more variety in taste because they did not salt everything. They had also found unique ways of treating certain plants — ways worked out, perhaps, through hundreds of years of experiments.

Roots

Roots are the smallest item, for the juicy ones, good for eating, grow in marshy places very unlike the Southwest. That of the Blazing Star plant, found in the Rio Grande valley, seems to have served the Tewa as food, but the others were good mostly for flavoring. The little wild onion was boiled with meat stew. Milkweed was chewed for the gum, and a plant of the pea family for the sweet taste. The wild potato was used as a vegetable but it tasted so bitter that the Hopi and Zuni, who ate it raw, mixed a special kind of white clay in water and took a mouthful of it after every potato, to kill the taste. This was one of those adaptations which must have taken years of experimenting. Sometimes Pueblo women varied it by boiling both potatoes and clay in water.

A good many wild plants had leaves succulent enough to be used as greens. Chief of them was the Rocky Mountain Bee Plant, so important to the pueblos that it was sometimes mentioned in ceremonies, along with corn, beans and squash. Leaves and stalks of this tall, purple-flowered weed were boiled down into a black syrup which was used for painting pottery. Also, they could be eaten, though the strong coloring matter they contained stained the mouth black. Hardened cakes of the black paint were sometimes broken up and cooked as food in winter, when vegetables were scarce. In the spring, every pueblo could find some

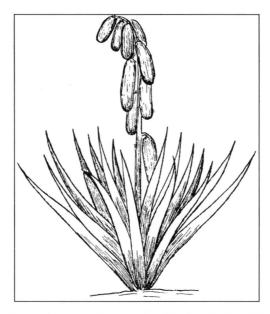

Broad leaved yucca. Drawing by Charles Shirley, Navajo.

sort of leaves that were juicy enough to cook and eat. So eager were they for this fresh food that they even boiled the sharp-tasting leaves of the young wild currant bushes and scraped the thorns from the prickly pear and the cane cactus.

Fruits

The list of fruits looks long but actually most of them are small and sour, with so little meat that the best way to treat them is to boil them, pits and all, and then grind them to a paste. Ground cherry and a berry of the nightshade family were treated in this way. Tomatillo was boiled and sometimes eaten with clay, like the wild potato. Juniper berries were heated in a pan (See page 50). Other small berries were eaten raw, even though the Hopi say that the wild currant made them ill. The only really meaty fruits were those of cactus and yucca. The prickly pear cactus, especially, has fruits almost as juicy as figs, after the long thorns are scraped off. Sometimes they were boiled and sometimes eaten raw (See page 54). The Hopi say that there was many a summer when they lived on these fruits, in the months before the corn ripened.

The banana-like fruit of the broad-leaved yucca, or Spanish bayonet, was the sweetest, and Pueblo women kept it the year round as their substitute for sugar and syrup. To get it ready for use was a two weeks' task. The fruit has a tough skin with plenty of seeds and fibre and women first baked it in a pit all night as they did sweet corn, to get it soft enough so these could be removed. The result was a sweet paste which they made into cakes and dried in the sun for a week or so. At Zuni, the women and their men relatives had a working ''bee'' at which they chewed the paste before setting it out to dry. After it had dried a little, they shaped and squeezed and rolled it, then dried it again, until they had smooth hard bars which they would keep for a year or so. When they needed sweetening for food, they broke off a piece and dissolved it in water, to form a syrup. The hard bars could also be nibbled without moistening and were a great delicacy.

Seeds

Seeds were the only plentiful wild crop, as they are in most dry countries. The Zuni, especially, have legends of the time before the Corn Maidens came, when all their flour was made of wild seeds. The way to cook them was to grind them to flour, mix with water and make into balls which were steamed on a support of twigs over a pot of boiling water. They still did this until recently with pigweed, wormwood, lambs quarters and cocklebur, though often they added cornmeal to the tiny amount of flour these small seeds produced.

Nuts

There were few kids of nuts, but one of them, the pine nut, was very important as food. These sweet nuts, growing between the leaves of some pine cones, are nourishing as meat to Indians lucky enough to get them. In California, they grow large and form one of the chief wild crops of the year. In pueblo country they are scarcely bigger than grains of wheat. The tree which bears them, in that region, is the scrubby little pinon

Pine nuts. Drawing by Charles Shirley, Navajo.

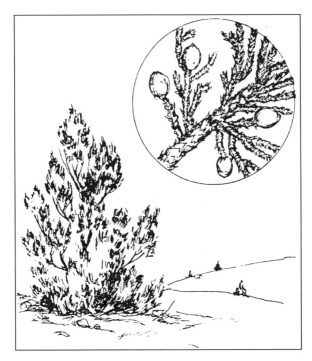

One seeded juniper. Drawing by Charles Shirley, Navajo.

(peenyone) which grows in the uplands. In late September, its cones begin
to fall, spreading out and spilling the nuts. Then in former days, whole
families went out to camp, working until snow came and gathering five
or six large baskets of nuts. They picked them up from the ground after
the cones had opened, threw the mass of nuts, earth and pine needles
on a winnowing tray (See page 37) and shook it to get out the trash, just
as they shook beans. Women brought the nuts back to camp in carrying
baskets on their backs and roasted them so that they would keep. In
roasting, they filled a large bowl or cooking jar half full of nuts, placed
it over a slow fire and stirred the nuts constantly so that they would not
burn. Nuts could be eaten raw also, but the toasted ones had a better taste.

Some Pueblo families still go out to gather pine nuts and camp for as
long as a month. They use wagons and carry the nuts in large flour sacks,
six sacks making an average harvest for a family. Often they sell part of
their harvest to the neighbors and those who do not buy in this way may
even get nuts from the Navajo whose country is full of pinon trees. The
trees are not considered private property, even though they may be near
a village, and nut gatherers wander wherever they please.

Acorns were the other nut crop, but a scanty one. They are always
ground to a meal which is rinsed many times with water to take out the
bitter poisonous taste. Pueblo people found a few oak trees in the river

valleys near the Tewa villages and in the mountains near the Keres, but they seem to have known nothing about the grinding and rinsing method. That may have been one reason they used so few acorns. They simply roasted them in a pot as they did the pine nuts and only used them when food was scarce.

Besides these native nuts, Pueblo people who went buffalo hunting on the plains, could bring back walnuts from the Arkansas valley.

Fungi

The puffball fungus grew abundantly in wet places and Zuni women, particularly, gathered quantities for drying. Among the Rio Grande Pueblos the fungus growing on cottonwood trees was broiled while the Hopi cooked corn smut.

Flavoring

People found salt hard to get and often they cooked without it. On religious occasions this was the rule. There was no prohibition, however, against herb flavorings and Pueblo women had as many of these as any modern cook. They gathered the spicy leaves or flowers while fresh and hung them on the wall to dry. The roots were then ground.

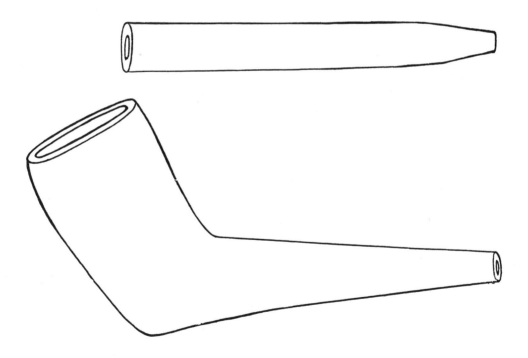

Shapes of pipes found in pueblo ruins, (After Morris).

Delicacies

Pueblo people, who had so few sweet things, enjoyed the sugary stems and even the flowers of some wild plants, which they ate raw.

Chewing Gum

Gum chewing is an ancient American custom, learned from the Indians. The pueblos chewed at least a half dozen plants, sometimes the dried sap as with milkweed and chicory, sometimes a juicy plant with tallow, as with cattail.

Beverages

Teas can be made by steeping the leaves of various spicy plants in hot water. Pueblo people made teas from leaves, flowers and berries and also a drink from sprouted corn which they claim was not alcoholic.

Smoking

Smoking was not a mere pleasure like chewing, for the blue clouds it made, so much like rain clouds, were used mostly by priests in ceremonies. Boys were not expected to smoke at all. At Isleta, they must kill a coyote (which meant a Navajo) before they could do so; at Santa Clara they must show they were grown hunters by killing the real animals, coyote, jack rabbit, deer and buffalo. If they disobeyed, they were thrown into the river. Even if they had a right to smoke, they must not do so before the older people until they were married.

One kind of native tobacco grew wild near some of the pueblos. Perhaps they traded for another kind from further south. They often smoked it in cornhusk cigarettes and sometimes mixed the tobacco with other dried leaves whose odor was thought to be especially sacred. One of these was mullen which Anglo children now place in cornhusk cigarettes, before they are allowed to use tobacco. They do not know that they are following an old practice of Hopi medicine men.

Pueblo people also used pipes and must have done so from the time of the Anasazi since pipes are found in the ancient ruins. They do not have the bowl and stem separate like modern pipes but are simply tubes of stone or of polished black pottery. Sometimes they are thicker at the center, so that they have the shape of a cigar, sometimes bent at right angles like the one in the picture. The pottery pipes have one end flattened for a lip piece, the stone ones have a wooden lip piece fitted on.

Indian Tobacco

WILD PLANTS USED BY PUEBLO PEOPLE

In the following list, the middle column contains the common names. However, since these vary or may not be known at all, the botanical names have been placed in the first column, arranged alphabetically for reference. All plants were not used in all pueblos, since climate and soil conditions were often quite different. Therefore, the third column contains initials of the pueblos where we know a plant to have been used. Abbreviations are:

A	Acoma	RT	Rio Grande Tewa
C	Cochiti	SA	Santa Ana
H	Hopi	SC	Santa Clara
HH	Hano, the Tewa	SD	Santo Domingo
	settlement on	SF	San Felipe
	Hopi 1st Mesa	SI	San Ildefonso
I	Isleta	T	Taos
J	Jemez	Zi	Zia
L	Laguna	Zu	Zuni

Plants Used for Roots

Asclepias galioides	Milkweed	J
Allium deserticola	Wild Onion	H HH
Recurvatum	Wild Onion	RT
Astragalus pictus filifola	Plant of Pea family	
	Milk Vetch	H
Cyperus inflexus	Sedge	A L
Laciniaria punctata	Blazing Star	RT
Petalostemon oligophyllus	Prairie Clover (eat raw,	
	also dry and grind)	A L SF
Solanum jamesii	Wild Potato	H RT
Solanum fendleri	Wild Potato	Zu
Acanthochiton wrightii	Pigweed	H
Amaranthus retroflexus		
Amaranthus blitoides	Amaranth, Pigweed	A C HH
		J L
Amaranthus graecizans	Amaranth, Pigweed	C
Artemisia dracunculoides	Wormwood	H
Astragalus diphysus	Wild Pea (pods)	A J L Zu
Atriplex nuttallii	Saltbush	I
Atriplex philometra	Saltbush	A C L

Chenopodium leptophyllum	Lamb's Quarters	H RK RT Z
Chenopodium incanum	Lamb's Quarters	
Cleome serrulata (also known as Peritoma serulatum)	Rocky Mountain Bee Plant	A H HH L RT Zu
Chrysothamnus confinis	Rabbit Brush (young buds)	A L
Echinocereus fendleri	Hedgehog Cactus	C
Lachtua integrata	Prickly Lettuce	A L
Mamillaria sp.	Ball Cactus	RT
Monarda menthaefolia	Horsemint	HH
Optunia polyacantha	Prickly Pear	A H L SF Z
Optunia arborescens	Cane Cactus	A L
Polyomintha incana	Mint	H
Portulca oleracea	Purslane	RT
Ribes inebrians	Wild Currant	Zu
Rumex hymenosepalus	Dock (Canaigre)	
Rumex venosus	Winged Dock	SF
Rumex mexicanus	Willow-leaved Dock	C
Sophia pinnata	Tansy Mustard	H RT
Stanleya albescens, pinnata, integrifolia	Mustard	H
Taraxacum taraxacum	Dandelion	RT
Typha latifolia	Cattail (eat root raw)	A L
Yucca glauca	Banana Yucca (young set pods boiled like string beans and eaten cold)	Zu

Prickly pear. Drawing by Charles Shirley, Navajo.

Fruits

Amelanchier prunifolia	Service Berry	I
Atriplex nuttalli	Saltbush Berry	A L
Bossekia parviflora	Thimbleberry	J
Ceanothus fendleri	Buckthorn Berry	A L
Echinocereus fendleri	Hedgehog Cactus	A H L
Echinocereus triglochidiatus	Hedgehog Cactus (pulp baked like squash)	I
Fragaria bracteata	Wild Strawberry (rare)	C I
Juniperus monosperma	One-seeded Juniper	C J L RT Zu
Juniperus pachyphloea	Alligator Juniper	I SF
Lycium pallidum	Tomatillo (Hopi eat with clay like wild potato)	A H J L RT Zu
Opuntia arborescens	Cane Cactus (cholla)	HH
Opuntia camanchica	Prickly Pear	RT
Opuntia clavata	Cholla (choya) (Sometimes dried, ground and mixed with cornmeal)	A L SF
Opuntia polyacantha	Prickly Pear	H
Opuntia whipplei	Prickly Pear	H Z
Padus melanocarpa	Chokeberry	A C L SF T
Physalis neomexicana	Ground Cherry	A L RT SF
Physalis fendleri	Ground Cherry	Z
Prunus americanus	Wild Plum	I T
Ribes inebrians	Wild Currant	A H L RT Zu
Rosa arizonica	Wild Rose	H
Rhus trilobata	Three-leaved Sumac	A H L RT
Smilacina amphlexicanulis	False Solomon's Seal	RT
Solanum triflorum	Nightshade (the Zuni boiled the bitter berries, ground them up and mixed with chile and salt as a relish)	A L Zu
Vitis arizonica	Wild Grape	A I J L
Yucca baccata	Spanish Bayonet	H Keres RT Zu

Seeds

Amaranthus	Pigweed	A H L Zu
Artemisia wrightii	Wormwood	Zu
Atriplex powellii	Goosefoot or Salt Bush	Zu
Chamaesaracha coronopus		H
Chenopodium cornutum	Lamb's Quarters	H
Chenopodium leptophyllum	Lamb's Quarters	Zu
Cleome serrulata	Rocky Mountain Bee Plant	A I L
Cycloloma atriplicifolium	Winged Pigweed	Zu
Eriocoma cuspidata	Indian Millet	H Zu
Helianthus	Sunflower	All pueblos
Koeleria cristata	June-grass	I
Lathyrus decaphyllus	Wild Pea	A C L
Mentzelia albicaulis		H
Mentzelia multiflora		H
Oryzopsis hymenioides	Indian Millet or Sand bunch-grass	H Zu
Sporobalus airoides	Alkali Zacaton	H
Sporobalus giganteus	Giant Dropseed	H
Sporobalus flexuosus	Dropseed	H
Vicia americana	Vetch (boil whole pod)	A L
Xanthium commune	Cocklebur	Zu

Nuts

Juglans major	Walnuts	RT (perhaps others)
Pinus edulis	Pine-nut (pinon)	All pueblos
Quercus utahensis	Acorn	RT

Fungi

Lycoperdon spp.	Puffball	Zu
Polyporus harlowii	Bracket fungus on cottonwood	All on Rio Grande
Utsilago zeae	Corn Smut	H

Herb Flavorings

Abronia fragrans	Sand Verbena (ground root)	A L
Agastache neomexicana	Giant Hyssop (stem and leaf)	A L

Allium deserticola	Wild Onion (stem and bulb)	H
Berlandiera lyrata	A Sunflower (flowers)	A L
Juniperus monosperma	One-seeded Juniper (berries)	
Juniperus scopulorum	Rocky Mountain Juniper (berries)	A L
Lygodesmia grandiflora	Hawkweed	H
Mentha canadensis	Mint	H
Monarda menthaefolia	Horsemint or Pennyroyal	A H HH L SI

Leaves for Smoking

Abies concolor	Balsam Fir	H
Mentzelia multiflora		H
Nicotiana attenuata	Wild Tobacco	All pueblos
Onosmodium thapsus	Borrage	H
Pinus ponderosa	Western Yellowpine	H
Portulaca oleracea	Common Purslane	RT
Verbascum thapsus	Mullen (smoked with above in curing)	H

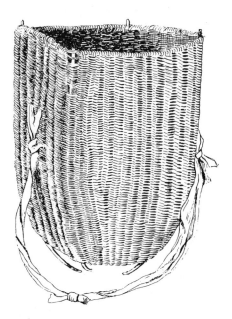

Hopi peach basket in wicker weave.

HUNTING THE MEAT SUPPLY

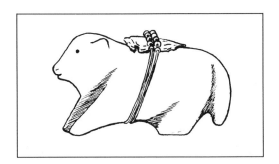

Zuni fetish, representing the mountain lion

For most of the year, the Pueblo people were vegetarians. They lived on the corn, beans and pumpkins in their storehouses, or what wild plants they could find. When they had meat, it was a special occasion. Still, there must have been much more game, in early days, than there is now, for old accounts speak of deer, antelope, mountain sheep, mountain lion, gray wolf, badger and fox. Pueblo people hunted all of these, for besides the meat they needed skin for clothing and for drums, sinew for bow strings, sewing and all kinds of fastenings, bone for tools and wall hooks, and hooves for rattles. In fact, there was no part of an animal which they did not utilize. Those who lived near the Plains, like Taos and Pecos, made long expeditions after buffalo and all the others went sometimes, even the distant Hopi. At home they could get small animals, like gophers and ground squirrels, but most of all the rabbit, chief animal food of all Indians in the Southwest.

Hunting often meant a long trip away from home and the best way to do it was for a number of men to work together. They would go to some place where they knew game was to be found, then drive the animals into a canyon or a roughly made corral where they could be easily killed. This kind of "surround hunt" or drive, was the usual thing with all American Indians before they had horses.

The Drive

It was a famous way to get deer, particularly when their meat was wanted for a ceremony, like the Taos deer dance, or for the yearly payment to the town chief, made by the Keres. Each pueblo had its own method, according to the lay of the country. The Hopi simply made a circle of men on foot around a place where deer were feeding. Two men entered the circle and drove the deer toward its rim, where the others shot them with bow and arrow. Pueblos which could get wood, like Zuni and Cochiti, built a huge fence and drove the deer inside it. The Zuni fence had openings at intervals and pits in the openings so that the deer, trying to escape, fell in and broke their legs. In order to get the deer inside the fence two men dressed like deer, with antlers on their heads; buckskin on their bodies; arms and legs painted white and short sticks in their hands so that they could go on all fours and seem to have front legs like a deer's. Deer do not have very good sight. They depend mostly on smell and if these decoys kept upwind so that no scent came from them, the deer would follow them, straight into the trap. Eastern pueblos sometimes imitated a deer call for this purpose by blowing into a hollow gourd with one hole in it.

Antelope were easier to get in quantity, since they travel in herds while deer feed by twos and threes. Moreover, a herd of antelope is easily stampeded and can be driven to the place where hunters are waiting. The Hopi, who live near open country where antelope are found, went to enormous trouble to accomplish this. They chose a place partly fenced in by hills and with trees nearby. There they built a corral of strong tree trunks with one opening. From this, long wings led out, fenced with brush for some distance and then marked by piles of brush for ten miles or so. Men stood along these wings to scare the antelope so that they would not try to leap the brush but would gallop down the open space into the corral.

When a herd was reported nearby, the boys of the village were sent to round them up. They got behind the animals and made a fire to frighten them. Then, as they began to move, the boys closed in around them, howling like wolves to make them run and driving them toward the corral. When they had entered it, the opening was closed with brush and good marksmen, standing outside the fence, they could shoot them as they milled around.

Mountain sheep were not so plentiful, yet travelers saw some near Hopi country in the 1880s. They too were surrounded but since they lived in such hilly places the hunters could often drive them over a precipice so that they would be killed by the fall. Those which got out on little points of rock were lassoed from above and hauled up to be killed. However the hunters always left a couple of these rare beasts, a male and a female, so that there would be sheep for another year.

Probably they hunted buffalo by the surround method also, stampeding the animals with fire or, in winter, driving them into deep snow, where they would flounder and be caught.

A surround hunt like this was a business venture, which might occupy all the men and boys of a village. It needed a leader, and most pueblos had such a man or perhaps a whole society of men, just as they had a war chief and a war society. These leaders must not only know the prac-

A buffalo dancer. Painting by Wo-Peen, San Ildefonso.

tical ways of getting game but they must know hunting magic. In fact, they were often more like priests than like business managers, for they had special songs and prayers that would coax the animals to them.

The best way of all to assure good fortune was to carry a little image of one of the beasts of prey, particularly Mountain Lion who had been a famous hunter, in the days when beasts were men. The tiny image, carved out of agate or turquoise, was blessed by a medicine man or a society. Modern hunters laughingly call a license a "Mountain Lion." Dead animals brought back to the pueblo were treated with great respect, so that their spirits would be pleased and send other animals for men's food. The bones were carefully put away and, sometimes, the bodies were decorated with blankets and turquoise. Deer whose meat was to be used for a ceremony, were killed without blood, by smothering.

The Rabbit Drive

Hunting for large animals was important, but it did not happen often. When the Pueblo people spoke of "the hunt" without any other description, they meant the hunt for rabbits. All the tribes of the Southwest have devised ways for collecting these little animals in quantity. The Paiute and southern California Indians put up long nets and drove the rabbits into them, where they could be killed with clubs. Pueblo people, for some reason, did not use the nets, but they made a specialty of rabbit clubs. These were not merely stout sticks, as they were in other parts of the country. They were flat, slightly curved pieces of wood which could be thrown for quite a distance. The Hopi clubs were the most elaborate and they have even been called boomerangs, like the curved throwing sticks of Australia. However, they do not come back to the thrower as some Australian sticks do (provided they don't hit anything), but after hitting, they bounce widely several times. A stick may hit the rabbit at which it is aimed and then, if the animals are coming thickly, strike several more as it bounces.

Other pueblos did not have the bouncing sticks of the Hopi but all had smooth heavy clubs which could be thrown a short distance or held in the hand for striking. To kill rabbits or other small beasts in this way saved valuable arrows.

All the pueblos had ceremonial rabbit hunts, when they wanted food for a feast, or for the ceremonial dancers, or, with the Keres, when the town chief or the war chief or the medicine societies needed meat to feed the sacred images. The arrangement was for the men of the town to go out under the regular hunt leader, make offerings and build a fire. This, said some of the pueblos, was so the rabbits would be blinded by the smoke. There were prayers and directions by the hunt leader and then the men formed two wings which gradually closed in a circle, throwing their clubs at every rabbit which started up.

When the hunt was less ceremonial, the women went along. This was a time as good for gaiety as the corn husking. The girls wore their best dresses and, at Cochiti, they carried toy rabbit sticks. They never carried real sticks or did any of the killing. However, they watched what the men did and as soon as they saw a rabbit fall, they rushed for it. The man who hit it, presented it to the first girl there and she, in turn, brought him a present of cooked food next day. At Hopi, this was a regular form of courtship.

Pueblo man throwing a rabbit stick.

The One-Man Hunt

Surround hunts were the usual thing when a quantity of meat was needed. However, a hunter might go out alone if he had time, or preferably two men together, to help each other and to carry the meat. These men, of course, could not surround the deer but they would find the tracks of one or two animals and follow them, sometimes running all day and all night.

The deer soon grew weak. It is a grazing animal, which has to spend long hours nibbling its green food as cattle do and when it had to run, with no chance to eat, it grew so feeble that the hunters could catch up with it. Sometimes they could even throw it down and smother it. Men who did this difficult kind of hunting were in special need of the little mountain lion image and few of them attempted the long run without it.

Trapping

Getting rabbits alone was a much simpler matter. Anyone, walking in open country was likely to scare one up and all men and boys carried rabbit sticks with them when they left the pueblo. If they did not see a rabbit, they might get a ground squirrel, rat or bird.

A surer way to catch these small creatures was trapping. Most pueblos used the form of trap called a deadfall, in which a stone was placed slant-wise and supported by an upright stick. Bait was fastened to the stick so that the animal, in nosing for the bait, would knock the stick down. The stone would then fall on the animal. Below is the diagram of a Hopi trap of this sort, for coyote and fox.

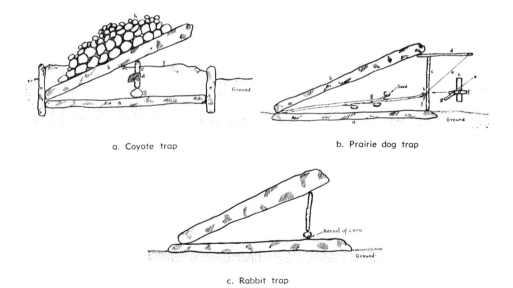

a. Coyote trap   b. Prairie dog trap

c. Rabbit trap

Traps for small animals.

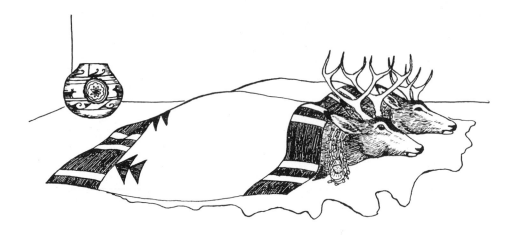

Honoring the dead deer, Zuni Pueblo. Drawing by Velino Herrera, Zia.

A is a flat stone, two feet square and eight inches thick, firmly placed in the earth. B is another stone of the same size standing at an angle. C is the small stick, 1 inch long, which holds up the slanting stone but without being fastened to it, so that the merest push would bring the whole arrangement down. D is bait tied to the stick. The hunter who set a trap like this would place a feather offering nearby, with a bit of turquoise to induce the animals to come. He sometimes does this today, even with steel traps. If he was catching such animals as rats, mice and prairie dogs he would not think the offering necessary, since these little creatures have no souls. For them he made a light trap, with a more delicate arrangement of sticks and stones than the larger one.

A and b are the two stones as above. C is the supporting stick. D is another stick lying across the top of c, between it and the slanting stone. To the end of d is tied a string, e, which is pulled tight and tied to the upright stick at f. The merest touch on this string will, of course, dislodge d and send the whole thing crashing down. In fact, a little more pressure is needed to keep it from falling in any case, so another stick, g, is wedged between the slanting stone and the upright stick. The pueblos did not do as much netting and snaring as some other Indians, perhaps because they were too much occupied with farming or because there were not so many small animals around their country. They had a way of catching prairie dogs without traps, by waiting until after a heavy rain and turning a stream of water into their holes to drown them out.

Animals As Pets

They also caught a good many birds, not for food, but for feathers. We have mentioned that their offerings to the gods were usually feathers attached to a string or, more often to a stick, in numbers of different ways. A Pueblo man could not have too many feathers in his possession and many men had special boxes, made of a hollowed chunk of cottonwood, for keeping this sacred property. They caught small birds in nooses made of human hair, which was invisible against the ground. A number of such nooses were attached to a stick laid on the ground. Then seeds were spread over the nooses to catch the feet of "all the birds of summer, rainbringers" when they stepped inside.

Eagle feathers were the most valuable of all and catching eagles was both a craft and ceremony. Eagles nest on the same high cliffs from year to year and, with the Hopi, each nest is the property of a clan. Four or five men of the clan go out in early summer, when there are young eaglets in the nests, not yet able to fly. They take offerings of prayer sticks, turquoise, cornmeal, a basket tray and a pottery bowl and leave them at a mountain shrine, dedicated to eagles. Then they go to the cliff and lower the lightest man or boy down over the edge to where the nest is. He picks one or two eaglets out of the nest with one hand and, with the other, fights off the father and mother in case they come back.

The other men have made small cradleboards out of rods and buckskin and in these the squawking eaglets are carried back like infants. In the village they are tied by one leg to the house roofs of clan members and the clan women wash them and give them names just as they would do to babies. They are fed every day on crushed meat, to make their feathers grow well, so rabbit hunts during the summer are a necessity. At the festival in August, called Niman, the eagles are killed by squeezing to death. The feathers are used for prayer sticks and for the costumes of sacred dancers. The bodies are buried in a special eagle cemetery.

When a clan did not own an eagle nest, there was another way to get the birds. A man would go out alone and build a little stone structure four feet high without a roof. Or else he would dig a shallow pit and, over it make a house of brush, like a small version of the houses built by the early people. He would make a roof of sticks and there he would tie a dead rabbit for bait. When the eagle swooped down to get the bait he would thrust his hand up through the sticks and catch the bird by the legs. Or, with the brush house, he might make a little door, get a live rabbit and tie it by the leg so that the rabbit was outside the door and the stick to which it was tied, inside. When an eagle came, the man had only to pull in the stick and drag in the bird, with its claws fast in the rabbit's body. In all these cases, the eagle was smothered by having its head pressed into the sand. Like the deer, it was used for ceremony and its blood must not be spilled. The eagle hunter had to make offerings, just as the nest robbers did.

All the pueblos used eagle feathers but none but the Hopi had nests owned by clans. Most of them caught young birds and kept them in cages where they could be seen as late as forty or fifty years ago. Only the Isleta people say they always shot their eagles instead of trapping them.

Another pet kept at many a house was the dog. He must have lived with the Anasazi for centuries for bones of dogs are found in very old

A Pueblo hunter, dressed in buckskin, Zia Pueblo. Drawing by Velino Herrera, Zia.

caves. They are short-legged animals which may have looked a little like a dachshund. They were not specially trained for hunting like a modern hound or a setter but they did go with the hunters sometimes. They may have been eaten when meat was scarce though dog meat was not a regular food in the pueblos as it was on the Plains.

The Anasazi also kept turkeys. Piles of the bones and dung of these birds are found in the old caves, so we know they must have had spaces, back of the cave dwellings, that were practically turkey coops. They probably caught the wild turkeys of the countryside and kept them there, but it does not look as though they ate them. Perhaps they were wanted only for feathers, as the eagles were, but turkey feathers were not used only for ceremonial purposes. They were twisted into ropes, as we shall see later, and made into cloth which must have been as warm as a down quilt. That, however, was long ago. The pueblo country now has few wild turkeys.

COOKING MEAT

Pueblo people ate every part of the animal except a little of the blood and perhaps some scraps which were left on the ground as an offering to Earth Mother or the beasts of prey. Those who criticize their diet because it was so largely cereal, must remember how many vitamins they got when they did eat meat.

If they ate meat in the hunting camp, they roasted it in the ashes or on a pointed stick stuck in the ground at an angle. In the village, the women cut it up and stewed it in a pot with coarsely ground corn or hominy, and some of the herbs mentioned. Meat which they wanted to keep was cut into thin slices, against the grain, and hung on a line to dry in the blazing Southwestern sun. This is the famous jerky. It is a pioneer's mispronouncement of a Peruvian Indian word which the Spanish wrote as charqui (charkee). It means sun-dried meat and has nothing to do with jerking. Treated in this way, venison, buffalo meat and the rest grew stiff as a board and would keep a long time in dry weather. When a woman wanted to use it, she soaked it in a pot of cold water, then boiled it.

Rabbits were too thin to be cut up in this way and they were generally skinned and roasted whole, then dried. Some of the Keres had men, officially appointed, who did the roasting. Sometimes they gave the intestines to the girls of the village for good luck.

Salt

We have talked about stewing meat with herbs and have said very little about salt. Yet salt was highly esteemed in the pueblos, so much so as to be holy. There was a legend that Salt Woman had passed their way in the long ago and, because her body was rough and scaly, no one would show her hospitality. Finally,˙ say some, a man from Laguna showed her kindness, though others say it was a man from Zuni. At least she said that she would go to a lake south of Zuni and there make her home and that people might come there with offerings to take the salt which is her body.

Zuni, Acoma and Laguna make yearly pilgrimages to this lake, Zuni led by the rain and war chiefs, Acoma by the Parrot clan and Laguna permitting the trip only to the Parrot and Pumpkin clans, with the town chiefs. They place offerings in the lake, ask Salt Woman's permission and then wade in reaching down for the salt with their hands. The lake is now leased by a commercial company, but a place is reserved where the Indians may keep on with their yearly ceremonies.

Some of the Hopi visit this lake too, but most of them go to their own salt spring in the canyon of the Little Colorado, near its junction with the Colorado River. It was the War Twins, famous in pueblo mythology, who placed their own grandmother here to be the Salt Woman and they gave the rules which all salt gatherers must follow. Any man may go on the two-day journey from Second Mesa but there must be an experienced man to lead, for the party must leave offerings at every spring and shrine they pass. On the way, they must eat only the ancient Hopi foods and they come back with omens as to scarcity or plenty next year according to what their leader sees in a mysterious cave, stronghold of Maasawu, god of the underworld.

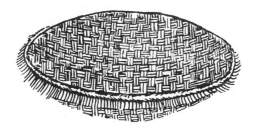

Yucca leaf winnowing tray. Drawing by Velino Herrera, Zia.

HOUSES AND FURNISHINGS

Roofs, ladders and chimney pots in Zuni

THE VILLAGE

SOLID AS THE PUEBLOS LOOK, they have not always stood just where they are now. Acoma, on its steep mesa and old Oraibi, on its low one are, perhaps, the only ones which occupy the very same positions as when the Spaniards first found them. Most of the others have moved — not far but enough to leave a trail of ruined sites behind them. Sometimes the reason for moving was the Rio Grande, which washed away church and fields at Santo Domingo one year. Sometimes it was the Spaniards, who threatened the Hopi so dangerously that several villages moved from the plain up to the mesa tops. Even villages which remained in the valleys, like the Zuni and Tewa, had hills of refuge, where they camped in time of war. When they came back, to re-build their crumbled houses, they often did so in a slightly different place.

Material for building lay at their feet. In the west, this was sandstone, the soft, red or yellow rock of which the mesas are formed. It splits so

Making adobe bricks.

easily that the men of Hopi, Zuni and Acoma could work it into smooth, thin blocks, even with their stone tools. They laid the stones up in walls a foot or so thick, filled the cracks with little stones and made them solid by plastering with mud. In the eastern river valleys, where stones were few, the whole house was made of earth.

But it was a special earth, the famous adobe, which covers so many thousand miles in Arizona and New Mexico. Adobe is a fortunate assemblage of clay and sand that dries hard but without cracking. In the absence of enough sand, the addition of straw will prevent the shrinkage and cracks that destroy its usefulness as a building material. Long ago, the Pueblo people knew about it and some of their very early shelters were made of poles and brush, covered thickly with adobe which dried as hard as stucco. When they began to build square houses, the eastern pueblos sometimes made theirs out of two rows of poles, set close together, with hardened adobe between them. If they could find small stones, they could even do without the supporting poles. In that case, they mixed the adobe with stones, much as people now mix cement with sand and stones for concrete. They built the stiff mixture up by handfuls to form a wall, letting each layer dry in the hot Southwestern sun, as a woman dries her pots while working. We might, in fact, think of this adobe house as a gigantic form of pottery. It would crumble in time but the householder had only to wait for the rainy season, when water was plentiful, and then mix some more.

Pueblo woman plastering the house wall.

Adobe was no surprise to the Spaniards and, in fact, it was they who gave it the name. The word sounds Indian but, actually, it comes from Arabia. So do many Spanish words, for Spain was conquered, at one time, by people from Africa, speaking an Arabian language. That is why, in the Southwest, we find many words and even customs which come, not from Indians nor from Europeans but from the people of Morocco.

The Spaniards, then, were acquainted with earth of this consistency and had been building with it for years in their own country. They, however, were used to shaping it into bricks, by forming it with wooden molds. They taught Pueblo people to build churches in this way and the archeologists in an old pueblo can tell if they come to a church wall because it will be made of bricks instead of the irregular-shaped handfuls used by the Indians. Soon Pueblo people learned to make bricks themselves and Now these are the regular thing for all houses built of adobe.

All that is recent, however. The pueblos, before the Spanish came, were built of adobe plastered against poles; adobe supported between walls of poles; adobe mixed with little stones; or finally, of stones cemented together with adobe. The style depended a good deal on the materials available. In any case, the walls were generally coated with a thin wash of adobe, to make them smooth and clean. Anyone who has seen the walls of Taos, clean as a picture for Saint Geronimo's Day, will know how fresh and bright this could make them look.

The villages, in those pre-conquest days, were usually in the apartment-house style, with one or more clusters of buildings, each three or four stories high. The Spaniards called them cities, yet actually each one held only about two hundred people, for the fields nearby would hardly have supported more. Each family was crowded into one room and the rooms were arranged in tiers, which rose one behind the other, like giant steps. The roofs of the ground floor houses made a balcony where people on the second floor could dry their vegetables, stack their firewood, make pottery and even cook. The roofs of the second story made a balcony for the third story, while the top story, which was probably the fourth or fifth, was free for all. There people could gather to watch the ceremonies in the public square below and there a village official could stand to call out announcements, as you may hear him do at Taos today.

This left many dark inner rooms on the lower floors, but they had their uses also. There were larger ones down into which families moved in the winter months, when fuel was scarce and their airy upper rooms hard to heat. There were others where priests retired to fast and where sacred objects were kept away from prying eyes. Most were used for storage where the village could pile up a year's supply of dried vegetables, "jerky," pottery clay, basketry materials and even firewood.

The Spaniards called this pyramidal building a fortress and it really served as one. There were very few window openings, for there was no glass before the Anglos came, and window frames were a problem to the ancient builders. In the bottom story there were no windows at all and the Spaniards who tried to attack it faced a solid wall, as unscalable as a precipice. Doors were almost as scarce. There were a few small ones leading off the balconies on the side away from the wind but, on the ground floor, none. Then how was the house entered? Through openings in the roofs, which were reached by ladders.

Every picture of an old-time pueblo is streaked with the slanting lines of ladders, leading from the ground to the first balcony, from that to the second and so on. That would be true at some time after the Spaniards arrived, but the early pueblos rarely had anything so convenient. Their ladder was simply a tree trunk with notches cut in it. Imagine a woman climbing such a pole, with a jar of water on her head, or a man, with a whole deer on his shoulders! Once up, they must climb down again, into the houses. The roofs were dotted with little square openings, like the hatchways which lead from the deck of a ship to its hold, and people often speak of these, too, as hatchways. Inside each was another notched log, which might be the only means of entering the one-room dwelling below.

No wonder women used to give feather offerings to the great Beings, so the Spanish accounts say, for luck in ladder-climbing. And no wonder that one of the favorite pueblo jokes was the talk of the bashful young man, coming to see his girl, who fell down the ladder and dropped everything. Yet ladders were convenient when the family did not want visitors, for then they could simply be removed. They must have saved the life of a pueblo more than once, when all ladders leading from the ground were pulled up, and the enemy left facing a blank wall.

Let us enter one of these ancient pueblo rooms, going, as the Zuni say, "up the ladder and down the ladder," for that was the regular expression meaning to enter a house. We will make the date of our visit about 1880, for that, as explained before, is about the time when the first anthropologists were writing their descriptions of the pueblos. Their pictures give us details about the pueblo way of life which the Spanish warriors never noticed.

We begin by going up the ladder to the first balcony, which is the roof of the ground story. Here, we find the floor covered with hard, well trodden earth, so thick that some fox skins are pegged out on it to dry. There are a few channels in it, made by the rainwater from the roof above, but these are mostly covered with flat stones to keep the roof from being cracked. There are even little spouts at the edge to carry off the water, though these are mostly flat stones, with now and then an old pot or a curved half of a gourd. Pueblo builders knew how to use anything they had at hand. Along the edge of the roof, there is a row of flat stones, laid along the tops of the walls, so the rain and sun will not crumble the masonry.

We find a hatchway leading into a dwelling room and see that the door is open. That is, the flat slab of sandstone which covers it in rainy weather has been removed and the ladder is in place. We cannot knock on such a door but we stand and call, hearing an answer from within. The family is at home. Feeling our way down the ladder, we find the room dark, except for a patch of sunlight from the hatchway and a flicker of firelight. The woman of the family is cooking at the corner fireplace. She wears her dark woolen manta dress belted with red and she is barefoot. White buckskin boots would be hot in the close room and when she squats in the soot of the fireplace, they would be dirty in ten minutes.

Her room, which is about 12 feet by 14, is the home of the whole family. Long experience, however, has taught them to make it both neat and convenient. The walls, which may be either of stone or adobe, have been neatly whitewashed. Whitewash is another of the riches of the Southwest, for there are dozens of deposits of gypsum where anyone may dig. The man of this family dug out the white crystals from a place he knew, brought them home on a donkey, and pounded them into fragments with a stone. His wife covered them with cattle dung and baked them, just as she would bake pottery, then ground them on a stone, like the one she uses for grinding corn. After the rainy season had come, when there was plenty of water, she moistened this whitewash and smeared it

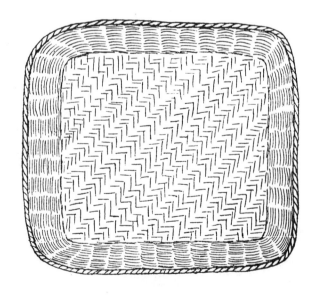

A yucca floor mat, Hopi Pueblo. Drawing by Velino Herrera, Zia.

over the wall with a piece of fur. Only around the floor she left what might be called a baseboard ten inches wide, which she plastered with brown adobe because floor dirt would soil the white.

We ask how long Pueblo people have been using this whitewash and she does not know. Perhaps the Spanish colonists found out about it, for all of them use it. Perhaps the pueblos always knew. Hopi, Zuni and some of the Keres are using it still. Many Rio Grande Pueblos buy it from the Spanish-Americans who bake it in a kitchen stove.

The floor of the room is of earth and, if this were a ground floor apartment, it would be simply a layer of mud, smeared over the level soil. If the room is on an upper story, the mud is smeared over the roof of the house beneath. We may wonder whether such a roof is strong enough in a country where there are no boards and few big logs for beams, but Pueblo builders, using all the materials they had, have worked out a very good system. Looking up to the smoke-blackened timbers of the roof above us, we can see what the first stages were.

When the walls were high enough the men of the family took donkeys (in former days they would have had to rely on their own shoulders) and went to the mountains for rafters. They got some straight cottonwood trunks, peeled off the bark, but did not try to square them up with their stone tools. They laid these rafters across the tops of the walls the short way and plastered them in with adobe mud, leaving the ends of the poles sticking out. One reason this room is no wider than twelve feet, is because it was so hard to get long tree trunks and to drag them to the pueblo.

It is much easier to get light poles from willows in the nearest canyon. The men cut plenty of these, getting them as long as possible. Then they peeled them and laid them across the ceiling beams, several inches or so apart. Looking up, you can see them and, above them, a layer of still lighter sticks, laid close together and going the other way. Then comes grass and brush going at right angles to the sticks. It is a series of at least four layers crossing one another, like laminated wood, which is made in just that way for strength.

Above the last layer came a heavy covering of earth which was evened and packed down by the people upstairs to serve as their balcony. The floor of the room where we stand, which is the roof of a storeroom below, was made in that same way. It looks almost as smooth as cement and the wife explains that, every rainy season, when she does her plastering, she gives it a thin wash of adobe mud. Some of the Keres do not mix their mud with water. They wait until they have killed a horse or a cow and then use the fresh blood which cakes like glue and makes a much harder floor. Our hostess says she also smooths over the outside of her house with this adobe mud, covering all the rough places, and every other year or so she whitewashes the inside. We can actually see the marks of

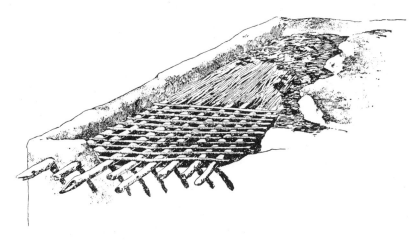

Construction of a roof.

her hands where she smoothed its uneven surface. Her sister next door does the same, but the sister whose husband is good at cutting sandstone has paved her floor with irregular stone blocks, the cracks between filled with adobe. Now she need not plaster her floor every year.

"And does not the stone make the floor too heavy for the room below?"

"Well, some clay and sticks shake down now and then, but that happens with all roofs."

It must, we can see, for this wooden roof is the weakest point of the house. In the ruined pueblos, hundreds of walls will be found intact, while almost every roof has rotted away.

Our hostess does not tell us of all the ceremony which went to the building of walls, floor and roof. Yet housebuilding is a matter for prayer and offerings, just as planting is. If it were a Hopi house — at least a ground-floor house — there would have been prayer feathers placed under the corner stones. Then the lines where the walls were to be, would have been marked out with food crumbs, sprinkled to the sound of an ancient house-building song. When the walls were up and the roof in place, more food crumbs would have been sprinkled along the rafters, to "feed" the house and bring health to those within it. Finally, some soft feathers would have been tied to one of the beams as an offering to the great Beings. Every November, at the Hopi New Year, the householder would renew this prayer for the dwelling's safety.

Other pueblos had various different ways of blessing the house. Zuni held and holds still, a great midwinter feast called the Shalako. Eight Zuni men volunteer to build big new houses each year to receive the masked gods which then visit the town. A husband and wife have to call on all their relatives to help build the new house and they pay them with food while they work. Then the gods dance in it all night and give it their blessing. This is the way most houses in Zuni are built and thus the whole town is a dedicated place, the actual home of the gods.

Windows and Doors

We have described the building as though it included no windows and doors, yet some rooms had them, even in quite ancient days. In fact, the room where we are visiting has a tiny window and an inside door. The window is a somewhat lopsided opening without a frame. The builders must simply have left a gap in the wall and placed several light poles across it side by side to support the wall above. We can see that the poles bent with the weight and do not wonder that the opening was made small and near the roof. It lets in some light, however. The opening is filled with slabs of selenite, a glassy variety of gypsum which fractures into slabs an inch or so thick. The builders have not tried to shape the slabs but have placed them side by side, held rigid with sticks, and the whole fixed in place with the useful adobe. This substitute for glass may be another hint that they got from the Spaniards. Several houses have such windows in the upper stories, which of course cannot be opened. Others have holes in the wall, sometimes closed with a rough wooden shutter, sometimes with a loose piece of wood or a stone. In cold weather they can be closed up with stones and adobe.

The door we can see goes into another one-room dwelling where the sister of the family lives. It is a small opening with sill at least ten inches from the floor. Yet it is more comfortable than many doors, for these are often made in T shape, the stem of the T at the bottom, the wide part beginning about at the waist of anyone going through. "Useful for a person carrying a load on his back," the pueblos say. Of course these doorways have no frames and no wooden doors. Often, as in this case, there is a wooden pole set into the masonry a few inches below the top of the door, and this serves as a curtain rod. Over it can be hung a skin or a reed mat and thus the apartments get privacy.

Furnishings

The furniture is mostly built in. Around two walls runs a masonry bench, which serves as a shelf or a place to sit on. In the wall are niches, one made by walling up an old door, others left when the house was built, and these serve as cupboards. A pair of deer horns and a wooden peg have been attached to the wall as clothes hangers.

On the floor, along one side of the room, is the most important furniture of all — three narrow bins, made of stone slabs. Inside each one is a grinding slab, the first of coarse lava, the next of coarse sandstone which is not quite so rough as lava and the third of fine sandstone. They are tilted up toward the wall and there is just space behind them for the girls of the family to kneel, facing the room. On the stones lie the cylindrical manos or hand stones, just the width of the slab, with which the grinding is done. Our hostess shows us how to kneel behind the first slab,

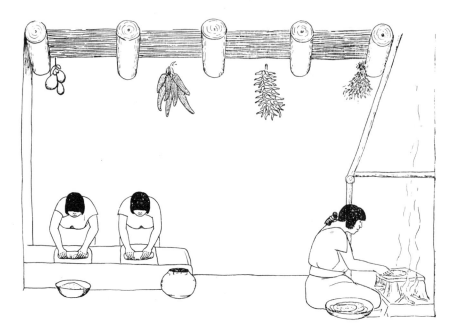

Pueblo women, grinding corn and making wafer bread.
Drawing by Velino Herrera, Zia.

pushing the hand stone up and down along the groove it has worn through years of work. The crushed kernels drop off at the end of the slab where they are caught by the sides of the bin.

"But that is a modern convenience," she explains, "or modern within two or three hundred years. Really old-time women just put a basket at the foot of the grinding slab."

"Does everyone use three slabs like this?"

"Oh no. My sister has four. But they are old ones that came from my mother. It is not easy to get good grinding slabs."

"How do you get them?"

"Why, you make them. Sometimes the men help."

She explains how her own husband kept a lookout for years for stones of the right size and roughness. He brought these three home one by one and chipped them roughly into shape. Then she, herself, worked at them for weeks, as a modern woman might work at her knitting, chipping at them with another stone until they were the right size and the right degree of roughness.

"Doesn't that leave some stone flakes which might get into the corn-meal?" we wonder, and she admits that it does seem to. But pueblo stomachs are used to that. So are pueblo teeth, some of which show the effects.

Now she leads us to the corner fireplace and the chimney which, also, she built herself. She does not know, any more than we do, whether the original idea came from Spain, but she remembers that, in very old times, there was no such thing. The fire in those days used to be in a hollow in the middle of the floor and the smoke went out through the hatchway. Not so good for anyone coming down the ladder.

Now fireplaces and chimney are in a corner and this, we gather, is because it is easier to build there, with two walls to give support, than if built just against one wall. She planned for the chimney when the wall was being built, for then a heavy pole was built in across the corner, about three feet from the floor, to serve as a support for the flue. Under it, she dug a hollow in the earthen floor, which was to be her fireplace, and directly over that, made a hole in the roof where the smoke would go out. Then she built the flue. Having no metal pipe or firebrick, she used what she had, basketry materials, covered with clay.

She placed an upright row of light sticks standing on the corner pole and slanting upward until they converged around the smokehole and she daubed them in place with adobe mud. Some women even weave them together, like wickerwork. When this framework was ready, she plastered it on both sides with handfuls of mud so that it formed a canopy which leads the smoke from fireplace to roofhole. Of course, with a hot fire, the adobe would crack off in chunks and the framework might burn. But she rarely has a hot fire. Fuel is scarce in pueblo country and the flame is fed with tiny sticks, over which the pot simmers slowly. The family keeps warm largely by the warmth of gathered bodies.

Above the smokehole, on the house roof, she has built a chimney. For this, she used a number of old water jars, with the bottoms smashed out. Piled one above another and cemented with adobe, they are as useful as concrete pipe. All over the roofs we can see similar chimneys, some high, some low, according to what materials the women had or determined by the height needed to "draw."

Inside, our hostess shows her cooking arrangements. Most of her food is stewed, so the main need is a support for the pot. She has built one, in the shape of three knobs of hardened adobe, a few inches high, in the bed of the fireplace. Some women prefer stones, which are movable, and some build little clay walls.

There is no other furniture in the room except two or three rough wooden blocks which the older members of the family use to sit on. These are a luxury since most Pueblo people simply unwrap the blankets which they wear for warmth, and fold them up as seats. At mealtimes, they squat on these around the stew pot on the floor. At night they stretch out in a row, wrapped in the same blankets with the addition of some larger ones and perhaps some rabbit skin robes. This bedding now hangs from

Gourds used as kitchen ware.

a peeled cottonwood pole, suspended from the rafters by yucca fiber string. Every house has such a "pole of soft goods" which serves instead of a closet.

The dishes and kitchen utensils are mostly on the floor. Beside the fireplace is the blackened cooking pot where the housewife stews her meat and vegetables. She has also a gourd dipper and two or three containers made by slicing the top off a gourd when it was fresh, then letting it dry and scooping out the seeds and pulp. The bulbous bottom and long neck of a gourd make it an excellent bottle and the first European settlers of American grew them for this purpose just as Indians did. In the niches are the bowls for mixing and serving food and, in a rack made of sticks, the painted jars in which the girls of the family bring water.

Besides these dishes, she has a mortar for pounding up food such as dried fruits. It is made of a lump of stone with a hollow in the middle, and the pounder is a smooth stone with a rounded end. By the hearth stands the bunch of grama grass which is used as a broom, while its small end, which does not touch the floor, serves as brush and comb for the family's hair. In a niche lies a torch, which is used on those nights when the family does not go to bed at dark. It is a heavy wad of cedar bark tied up with yucca strings. Fire will smoulder in such a torch for a long time, and warriors carried it with them in the days when they had no matches. When the Hopi of Walpi put an end to the "traitors" at neighboring Awatobi, it is said that they lit such torches as this and flung them down blazing into the ceremonial room where the Awatobi men were gathered. Actually, recent excavations at Awatobi do not bear out the legend.

In former times, torches were lit at the fire and when the family traveled, someone carried a smoldering torch to light the next fire. They had firemaking tools too, and our hostess gets the old one from the storeroom to show us. It is a round stick of soft wood in which little hollows have been drilled at intervals. The man of the family placed some shredded cedar bark in one of these hollows, then took another short stick of hard wood with pointed end, which he placed upright in the hollow and twirled rapidly between his palms. In a minute or two a spark would fall into the cedar bark and the women would have another bunch of bark ready to catch it and take fire. After the white settlers came, they learned to strike fire with flint and steel, as seventeenth century Europeans did.

This completes the household equipment, except for what is in the dark storeroom below. The woman of the family does not do all her work in her own dwelling. She is continually running up and down the ladder to outside ovens and drying racks. Out on the balcony, she and the other women of her family have what they call their *piki* room, where they make the famous wafer bread, of blue cornmeal (See page 42). This equipment, too, they made themselves.

Ancient pueblo pottery dishes.

They began with a chimney and hood, standing in a sheltered corner of the balcony, where a house wall juts out. "Though some women," she explains, "build them in inner rooms, in alcoves — anywhere they can get space." Under the chimney hood is the nearest approach to a stove that the pueblos had. This is an oblong stone, mounted on two long low ridges of clay, so that a little tunnel is formed under it. In this tunnel the fire is placed where it is protected from drafts and can heat the oven like a griddle.

It sounds simple, but the stone which can serve such a purpose must have been through a long preparation. It must be smooth sandstone to begin with, then its surface must be soaked with oil, generally from sunflower or squash seeds, though buffalo fat is good if you can get it. Our hostess and her sisters used squash seeds which they chewed and spit out on the stone, after it had been gradually heated. It was a ticklish business for if the temperature were changed suddenly, the stone would crack. At least, that is how we interpret it. But the explanation of our hostess is: "The stone cracks if anyone speaks out loud. Sometimes it does so anyway and then we know some woman must have a bad heart."

It took them almost a day to get the stone properly heated, rub the squash oil into it and then rub it again with wads of pinon gum, which melted and sank into the pores. They finished by scrubbing the stone with juniper and pine twigs, which left it clean and slightly scented. When it is wanted for *piki*, it must again be gently heated.

There is more kitchen apparatus on the balcony, for several of the women have built racks of poles there for drying meat and vegetables. One woman has even dug a pit where she can do fireless cooking, building up the pit sides with stones, since she could not dig too deep into the ceiling of the house below. Most of the pits and the Spanish-type ovens are down on the ground and we realize, clambering down to them, what a space a woman had to cover in her activities, even though she did live in one room.

The cooking pits and beehive ovens, scattered through what we might call the pueblo front yard, all work on the same principle. We have already mentioned this type of fireless cooking. Fire was made in the enclosed space and left to burn out. Then, when the space was well warmed, the food was put in, sealed up and left to cook slowly. A fine way to conserve vitamins, say the dieticians, and it was a way practiced, in some form, by most of the Indians of America.

Our pueblo has two forms of pit ovens. One, which our hostess calls very old fashioned, is simply a hole dug in the ground, about a foot wide and eighteen inches deep. She leads us to one which has the floor and walls plastered with clay, baked hard by the many fires which have burned there. Beside it lies the flat stone which is used to cover it when

A Pueblo woman at her mealing bin.

the food is cooking. The Hopi women, she has heard, dig little side vents for their earth ovens. Then, when they are cooking the special corn mush for which Hopi is so famous, they can stick their hands down through the side tunnel to feel how the cooking goes, without uncovering the top.

The favorite, newer form of oven is the "beehive." The pueblos call it by the Spanish name, *horno*. Many researchers think, in fact, that it was Spaniards who showed the pueblos how to make this oven, for it is exactly like those used in Spain and France hundreds of years ago. In fact you can see examples of it in Europe still.

Our hostess built her own, which is about four feet high, made of stones plastered together with adobe. At one side, she left a door, about a foot a foot and a half square. This is just large enough to admit the flat wooden shovel on which she places her wheaten loaves. Toward the top, she left a smaller hole, large enough to admit her hand. Then she plastered the whole thing with adobe, inside and out, just as she plasters her house every year. The big door is closed now, for the oven is not in use.

"If it were open, the dogs would be in it all the time," she explains, "and our children too."

She has been lucky enough to get an old sheet of galvanized iron, which is held against the door with stones. "Much better than in the old days," she says, "for then we had to fill the doorway with stones and clay every time we closed the oven."

Looking along the house fronts, we can see that almost every family must have an oven of this sort for they are dotted everywhere, some on the ground and some on the balconies. Near them, against the houses, stand scaffoldings of poles and these, our hostess tells, are for drying meat and vegetables. Drying is the regular pueblo way of preserving food and at harvest time, or after a hunt, these racks are full for weeks at a time. Larger racks are for holding firewood. There are few trees near any of the pueblos and the men have to go long distances to get their winter fuel.

We can see a woman now, bringing in an armful for her cooking fire. Another is taking loaves from her beehive oven. Through an opening, on a balcony we can see two others working over their special stove for wafer bread constructed in an alcove. On another part of the balcony, a woman is brushing her daughter's hair, while another sits making a winnowing tray. This "front yard" of the pueblo serves as an outdoor kitchen and sitting room too. Pueblo people may be city dwellers but their windowless rooms are used mostly for sleeping and for shelter in bad weather. Their regular daily life is out of doors.

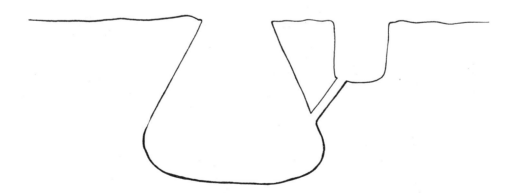

Outline of Hopi pit oven, with vent.

A Pueblo woman building a beehive oven.

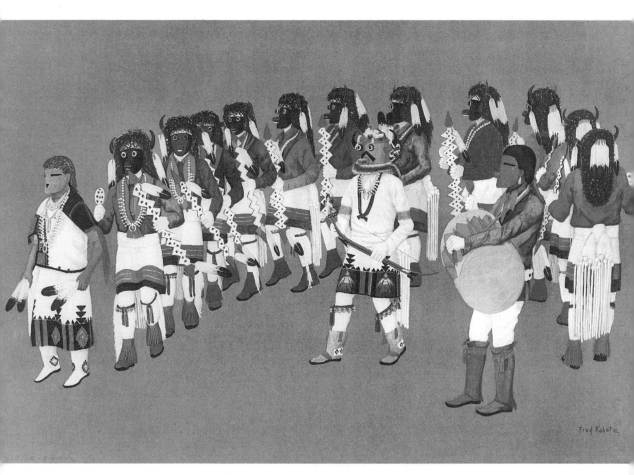

"Buffalo Ceremony." Painting by Fred Kabotie.

We notice other structures in the "front yard" but our hostess leads us in such a way that we do not directly pass them. These are the ceremonial rooms, known by the Hopi name of kiva (keeva). In the Hopi villages or in Taos and Picuris, we recognize them only by the long ladders, reaching up, apparently from underground. With some of the Tewa, they are circular buildings above ground but with a ladder or even stairs, going up to the roof entrance. In Jemez, Zuni and many other pueblos, you could not recognize them at all, for they are simply rooms in the house cluster.

No one could speak of the great apartment house villages, or even of twentieth century pueblos, changing so fast to look like Spanish towns, without noting these sacred rooms, or churches, so important in Pueblo life. The kiva must have come down from very ancient days, for it reminds us often of the circular houses of the Anasazi, dug into the ground and roofed with poles. Perhaps Pueblo people had ceremonies in such houses long ago and, as they changed their dwelling houses, building them square and above-ground, they still kept this ancient "pit house" for ceremonies.

Strangers visiting a pueblo should walk carefully where they see a ladder projecting out of the ground or out of a circular building. This is a sacred place, closed to visitors. However, the pueblos vary in their feeling about its exclusiveness. The Hopi do not feel that a church need be kept separate from daily activities. They hold religious ceremonies in their kivas but also, groups of men meet there to weave or spin or talk. Sometimes they have been willing to take visitors in, if these were people they trusted. Tanoans, on the other hand, prefer to keep the church as a specially sacred place. They reserve the kiva for religious ceremonies, they do not invite visitors and some of them even feel that it is impolite for strangers to walk past it.

CLOTHING
AND STYLE CHANGES

Ancient ceremonial dress.

Modernized dress worn by
singers at ceremonies.

Pueblo people were almost the only Indians in the United States
to have garments made of cloth. While other tribes were dressing in
skins, these farmers were growing cotton, spinning it, dyeing it and
weaving it into clothing. Only one other group above the present Mexican border did this to any extent — the Pima and Papago of Arizona.

Yet the pueblos did not always weave. Through the fifteen hundred
years that we know them to have lived in the same general country,
they have changed the make of each garment at least once. Some they
changed several times, as new materials came in.

Ruins show that, in the earliest days the Anasazi wore animal skins,
if they could get them. More often, they dressed in bark or fibre. Indians
on the lower Colorado used willow bark. Those of the Basin, to the

north, were reduced to sage bark. Those in pueblo country took the long tough leaves of the yucca, the same plant which furnished them with basketry materials and hair shampoo. They tore these into strips to make a skirt for the women, which was nothing more than a knee-length fringe, hanging from her waist. The man had a breechcloth of strips woven together like basketry. On their feet they wore sandals, which were flat soles at first twined, of Indian hemp, then plaited, of yucca strips.

They needed wraps for the winter but they had no large animal furs, such as bear, buffalo or even beaver. So they took the small skins of rabbits and later, turkey feathers, made them into long, fluffy ropes and twined them with yucca string into a sort of cloth. The process, described elsewhere, was not really weaving but rather basketry, with soft materials. The Anasazi must have begun this very early, for there are scraps of fur and feather cloth in ruins dating probably before 500 A.D. They even kept tame turkeys, and probably their need for feathers was one of the main reasons. Long after they began to weave cotton this old style of wrap was popular and did not begin to be abandoned until the Spanish brought them wool which was just as warm. They ceased to keep tame turkeys long ago and the feather blankets disappeared but there were still plenty of rabbit skins from the community hunt and travelers fifty or sixty years ago could still see a rabbit fur blanket or two.

By at least 800 A.D., most of the pueblos were wearing cotton. We do not know how they learned about it, though we guess that the news may have traveled up from the south where Mexico and Peru had weavers as skilled as any in the world. Not all of them took up the new material. North of Cochiti the climate was too cold to grow cotton and people had to trade for it. Some of these northern pueblos, like Taos and Picuris, had no temptation to trade, for they were on the edge of the Plains where they could easily get skins. Many wore buckskin clothing, but the majority had cotton, shaped into the very garments worn in ceremonies to this day.

The picture on page 91 shows a Tewa man and woman dressed in such garments for the Corn Dance. Forget the decoration, which is modern, and look at the shape. There are no sleeves or trousers, in fact, no sewing at all. Each person wears simply a strip of material, wrapped around the body and fastened at the waist by a sash. The man has a narrow strip, reaching from the waist to the knee, the woman a wider one which passes under the left arm and is fastened on the right shoulder, with the two edges hanging down the right side. It was a convenient form of clothing where there were no scissors for tailoring and probably not very good needles. The weaver simply made a piece of cloth, wide

Man and woman dressed for a Rio Grande ceremonial dance.
Drawing by Velino Herrera, Zia.

or narrow and as long as the wearer needed and the wearer belted it on. No fittings, no hooks, no buttons.

There was very little color, either. That is hard to imagine, if one has seen a modern pueblo ceremony, blazing with turquoise and yellow, indigo and scarlet. Pueblo people love color but, in the early days, when their dyes were made from plants or from colored earth, they found bright shades almost impossible to obtain. Scraps of garments found in the ruins show that they may have had a brownish red, like that made today from mountain mahogany. Then there was mustard yellow, perhaps from rabbit brush and faint blue, from blue beans or larkspur. Among mineral colors, they had brownish red and yellow from ochreous clay and one bright color — the beautiful blue-green made from copper sulphate. That turquoise blue is still made today, for no chemical dyes can duplicate its deep, glowing shade.

As a rule, the garments must have been of yellowish white, the natural color of cotton. At least, they were white to begin with but they had hard wear and water was scarce. After awhile, they must have turned to gray and brown. Still, they were precious. Scraps found in the ruins are patched and re-patched, showing that their owners wore them as long as they would hold together. The mending is done with coarse cotton or sinew and a bone needle, and there is no attempt to use a piece of fabric that will match. Any piece of fabric in those days must have been a luxury. Probably its owner never had but one cotton garment in all his life, but even so felt superior to those who wore only bark and skins.

Most people went barefoot, except when they made long journeys. Then they wore the ancient footgear of the Southwest, the sandal. This meant a flat sole, woven of yucca and tied to the foot with yucca string. It had been the footwear in pueblo country from early Basketmaker days and it was made by the early method — basketry. This may seem a surprising idea to those who think of all Indians as wearing moccasins. Yet basketry was the main source of equipment for the early Anasazi and they worked wonders with it. The caves show oval-shaped soles, heavy and strong as the lids of baskets. They show fine ones, with colored designs, and coarse ones with fringed bottoms, to be used in rough country. They show sandals twined and twilled and woven. In fact, there are so many styles that archeologists can tell a great deal about the date of a ruin, simply from the sandals found there.

In some of the later caves, there are moccasins. We do not know when Pueblo people first began to use these and we guess that the few who lived in good hunting country had skin footwear from a very early date. But moccasins did not come into regular use until some time after 1300. Why the change? We guess that it came about in the same way as the change from wild seeds to corn or yucca fibre to cotton. Pueblo people had met some new neighbors and learned how to use a new material.

Were the newcomers the first of the Apache, arriving from the north? Or were they Navajo, Paiute or Walapai, all of whom wear moccasins of the same peculiar type. For it *is* a peculiar type. Look at the next one you see and notice how tall it is. With a man, it comes above the ankle, with a woman, to the knee, while other Indian moccasins are mere slippers. Look at the sole. It is not flat, like the sole of a shoe, but turned up for an inch and a half, all around the foot and crinkled into place, like the sole of a sneaker or a rubber boot. No native Americans wear moccasins of this sort except those of the Southwest and the Eskimo.

If you are interested in Indian history, you have a fascinating problem here, and do not be surprised that it hangs on such a simple thing as the make of a moccasin. Is this odd, tall moccasin a pueblo invention? We can imagine the Pueblo people getting some new, large pieces of buckskin from their hunting neighbors. They might wrap their legs in the buckskin and then tie the sandals on outside it. Finally, they might sew the two parts together, turning up the soles on the sandals, which were always made large. Or, they might have got the whole moccasin from the newcomers. Navajo and Apache come from a land where the Indians wear tall moccasins, though with soft soles. If these were combined with sandals, that gives us a picture of how the styles of two peoples were combined to make a new invention. But the Spaniards wore soft leather boots which flopped around their calves much as the boots of Pueblo women do now. Perhaps all the Southwest learned from the Spaniards, after the hunting Indians had brought in plenty of leather. Whatever the truth may be, it shows that there was movement and change in old pueblo times, as there is today.

Moccasin with turned up sole. Drawing by Velino Herrera, Zia.

Along with the moccasins, came buckskin leggings. These were a new style for Pueblo men, who usually wore a piece of material wrapped around their hips. Even when they had buckskin, they used it in this way and, at the Hopi snake dance, you may still see buckskin kilts, dyed and painted. Indians from the east, however, wore leggings — long, tube-like garments which were really trousers without the seat. They were hung from the belt by thongs and a breech cloth, front and back, supplied the rest of the covering. After they met the hunting tribes, Pueblo men, too, began to make these garments, especially in the eastern pueblos. You may see the war chief wearing them still at a Tewa ceremony.

We have carried the story of pueblo dress up to about 1600, when the Spaniards came to stay. We have seen that it consisted mostly of pieces of cotton, taken straight from the loom, unsewed and in their natural color. Men and women had begun to wear moccasins, some men had buckskin leggings and their warmest garment was still the fluffy blanket of rabbit skin. Then the Spaniards settled down, with their sheep and cattle. They began to weave wool and dye it as they had done in Spain. They began sending to Mexico City, then a flourishing Spanish capital, for cloth and silver and dyes and utensils. Pueblo people got some of these in trade or as pay for their work.

First of the new materials was wool. Now the Pueblo weavers could make large, warm blankets, to place beside their blankets of rabbitskin. They could use wool for the woman's blanket dress previously many a woman, shivered in winter in the cold upper rooms of the houses. They could use wool for bright new sashes and, sometimes, for men's breech cloths.

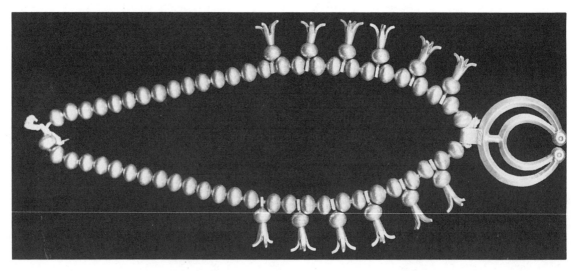

Silver squash blossom necklace, showing Spanish influence.

They made all these things and they made them in new colors. Perhaps the favorite among these was bright red, a shade hard to get with vegetable dye. The Spaniards were fond of it and the story is that Indians traded for the bright cloaks and trousers of the Spanish soldiers. They unravelled the worn cloth, re-spun the thread and used it in their own weaving. Soon bolts of red cloth were being shipped to the Southwest for trade. It came from Spain and was called by the Spanish name, *bayeta*, yet it was made in England.

Even in those days, England was a great commercial country and, while she was busy settling the eastern part of the United States, she was also selling goods to Spain to help settle the west. For years, the red English baize was shipped to Spain. Then it went by ship to Mexico and then, by caravan, up to Santa Fe, the Spanish capital in the Southwest. There, some lucky Indian would get hold of a piece, unravel it and spin it again more tightly. Finally he — or she — would use it as a border or

Striped Hopi Blanket.

Maiden's shawl, of white cotton with border in red and blue wool.

stripes in some fine garment. You can feel the soft texture of this old English baize in the borders of maiden's shawls made as late as fifty years ago. The center of such a shawl is of white pueblo cotton just as it was, perhaps, in early Spanish days.

Dark blue was another favorite color. It was made from indigo, a plant which grows in Mexico and it may be that the pueblos had been trading for it even before the Spaniards came. If so, they had only used it in small quantities for archeologists cannot be certain that anything they have found was dyed with indigo. The Spaniards, however, had used indigo in their own country. They wanted a great deal of dark blue cloth and they had their caravans bring dried indigo from Mexico in quantity. In making dye, they mixed the blue with urine, the only way to make the color permanent without modern chemicals. Pueblo people used the same method and some of their oldest blankets have stripes of deep dark blue. The color became so popular that some pueblos always made their women's dresses of dark blue and do to the present day.

These dresses are embroidered and some scholars are still wondering whether embroidery was learned from the Europeans or not. It is regrettable that the Spanish writers were men and soldiers who never bothered to notice how clothes were made. They speak of decorated dresses and certainly the decorated dresses seen in the pueblos now are embroidered magnificently in colored wool. Still, none of them date earlier than 1879. There is no embroidery in the ruins, though there is some patching and darning. And there are needles. They are slivers of bone or yucca thorn, much bigger than a modern darning needle but with a real eye in the butt end. They could have been used for large-scale embroidery but what was the thread? Red cedar fibre, perhaps, since there was no wool. Archeologists watch every scrap of material dug up, hoping to find the evidence.

Meantime, the striking patterns now seen on pueblo ceremonial costumes are done with steel needles and commercial yarns. But they are in ancient pueblo design. The terraces and angles are very much like those seen on coiled basketry showing that, even if the pueblos have taken over a new art, they have fitted it to their old style. It is handled according to old habits too, for the workers have usually been men, just as the weavers are. However, a new class of commercial embroiderers is coming into being and these are women. Some of them are placing their old designs on table linen and modern clothes for sale in tourist shops. Younger ones are being taught at the Indian schools to use the old patterns and stitches.

Knitting is another job for men. It was learned in early Spanish days, and the old reports tell how the pueblos used to knit hundreds of pairs of stockings to be sent with the caravans which went once a year to trade in Mexico. These stockings had no feet, perhaps because feet were hard to make and perhaps because the garments were needed more as leggings. Many Pueblo people used to wear them in cold weather and a few old men and an occasional woman knit them still.

Pueblo people learned sewing under Spanish rule, or rather tailoring and dressmaking. For a long time they had been fastening pieces of cloth or skin together by making a few holes with an awl and drawing a string or a leather thong through them. But it must have been the Spaniards who taught them the complicated art of making trousers, and

Embroidered white cotton robe.

shirts with sleeves, and the long dresses which women now wear under their mantas. For some time, men wore trousers rather short and slit to the knee in the old Spanish style. In fact, Indian men all over Mexico as well as the Southwest adopted this style and many of them wear it yet, though their trousers are white cotton instead of the velvet that the conquerors wore.

Then came the railroad, bringing calico and silk and, finally, commercial clothing. Today, when no ceremony is going on, Pueblo men wear modern clothing except for their heads and feet. The hair is often worn long, particularly with older men, since this is necessary for the dance costume and is often prescribed by religion. Even younger ones, with short hair, may put on a bright headband or kerchief instead of a hat, and you can tell by the headdress to which village a man belongs. On their feet they wear moccasins and some pueblos feel so strongly that this is a necessary part of their ways that they forbid shoes inside the village. Men who wear heeled shoes at least put a little cotton in them to keep connection with the ancient life.

Women, too, wear modern clothes, or at least the younger ones do. Older ones, especially in the western pueblos, still cling to the *manta* or blanket dress. They now often buy heavy blue or black commercially made cloth. They no longer leave the dress open down the right side but sew it down, decorating the seam with handmade silver buttons or pins. Under the *manta* they have an under dress of silk or cotton, perhaps in bright colors. Its long sleeves and lace skirt ruffle show beyond the *manta* in bright contrast.

Women in the eastern pueblos wear their ancient costume for corn dances but, on other days, if they wear *mantas* at all, they make them of bright colored silk or calico. Beneath, they wear the bright colored under dress and, over their shoulders, a bright silk shawl, hanging down the back and tied by its two ends around the neck.

The following pages give an itemized wardrobe for the Pueblo man and woman, at about the time when the villages were first studied by anthropologists. Yet even then, there must have been old fashioned people and progressive ones, just as there are now, and clothing must have been in several stages of development. The description of each garment has really to be a picture of its different stages, like a slow-moving fashion show.

MEN'S CLOTHING

Breechcloth

A strip of white cotton cloth, worn between the legs and passing over a belt, front and back. It was between 70 and 90 inches long and 16 to 18 inches wide. At Acoma, the ends were sometimes embroidered with geometric patterns in blue, with touches of red, green and brown. When wool came in, breechcloths were usually made of that material, in a dark shade but sometimes with colored strips.

Kilt

A strip of white cotton cloth wrapped around the hips like a very short skirt. Size about 32-45 inches by 17-20 inches. Along one of the short sides is a band of embroidery several inches wide in red, green and black, usually with standardized pyramidal designs representing rain clouds and parallel strips representing fields. This band starts at one long side but does not reach the other, the undecorated section being hidden, while in use, by the sash. Some kilts have additional decoration in the

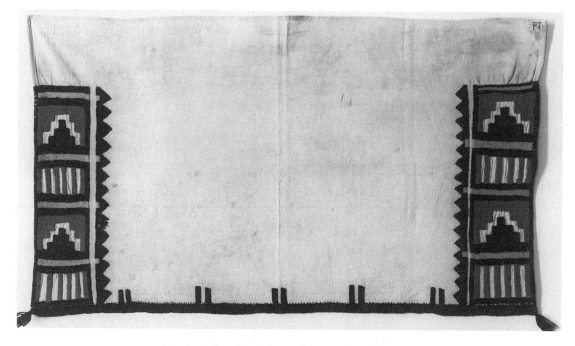

Man's embroidered dance kilt, Cochiti Pueblo.

form of a narrow black wool braided edging along the bottom. Some later kilts were made in wool and also in colors. A few kilts, like those used in the Hopi snake dance, are of buckskin, painted in earth colors. The modern ones have fringe tipped with little cones of tin which rattle as the weaver moves.

Sash, Brocaded

A strip of white wool cloth (rarely cotton) 2½-3 feet long and 6-8 inches wide. At each end is 6 to 8 inches of decoration in green and black, woven into the cloth by the method known as brocading. Below the brocading are long fringes.

Sash, Braided

Though commonly known as the "rain sash," Hopis call it the wedding sash. A strip of white cotton cloth 4-5 feet long and 4-8 inches wide, made by braiding, not weaving (See page 102). Each end has a heavy fringe of twisted cords 18-24 inches long, and where the fringe joins the cloth there are large, round knobs, of cotton string over a foundation of cornhusk. This sash may be one of the oldest forms of cotton garment, made before the loom was used, for one like it, even to the cornhusk knobs, has been found in an ancient cave. The old one is not so wide as the moderns and may have been for regular wear, to hold up the kilt, for which the present-day sashes are too elaborate. Many of the pueblos still braid this sash, even though they have given up regular weaving, for it is often a part of the man's dance costume. The Hopi call it a wedding sash and the bridegroom's family make it for the bride on her marriage. However, it is the men of her family who wear it, and then only for ceremonies.

Blanket

The woolen blanket, which gradually displaced the earlier ones of feather and fur string, was used, like them, both for robes and bedding. The first blankets had a simple pattern of stripes, running across the short way of the blanket. Sometimes there was a white background, with groups of dark stripes, at other times the whole blanket was of blue and black stripes, with an occasional light decorative one. You can see these same stripes in early Navajo blankets, which were probably copied from the pueblos. The Navajo went on to heavy rugs and new

Pueblo ceremonial sash.

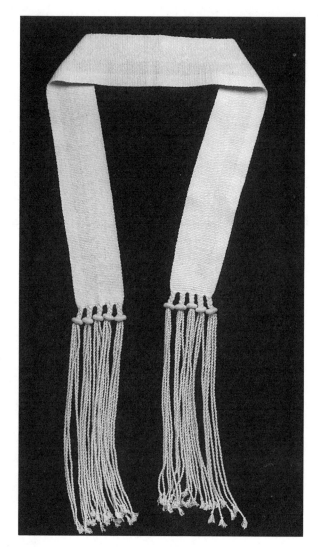

Braided "rain" sash, Hopi Pueblo.

patterns while the pueblos kept to their stripes until all but the Hopi ceased to make blankets. The Hopi, meantime, worked out an additional style, which is rather like a Scotch plaid in black and white. Only the Hopi make blankets now. Other pueblos trade for them with the Hopi or, more often, buy them from factories. Usually they like the brilliant fringed ones, in oriental patterns, but Taos men prefer those used for bedding: wool or cotton in pink and blue checks for winter, white sheeting in summer. Zuni men, for ceremonial occasions, insist on an all-black blanket.

Shirt

The shirt with sleeves is a modern garment, not made until after the conquest. Before that, the Pueblo man may have sometimes protected the upper part of his body with a plain strip of cloth with a hole in the middle. He put his head through the hole and the ends hung over his chest and back. Indians in Mexico and South America still wear this unsewed type of upper garment. It is known by the South American name, *poncho*. The poncho could easily be made into a sort of shirt if two pieces were attached to it at the shoulder to form sleeves. Old examples show that Pueblo people sometimes did do this but they did not sew the sleeves into tubes or sew them on. They tied pieces of cloth to the shoulders at one or two places and perhaps tied them together at the wrist.

We cannot tell when they first began to do this but Tesuque and San Juan people remember when such shirts were made of handwoven cotton, like the one in the picture shown on page 104. The Tesuque shirts were heavily embroidered with commercial yarn. Later, many pueblos made shirts in the same style but of blue wool, like the woman's dress. Also, occasionally, brown and black. After they began to get commercial cloth, they made white cotton shirts for dress-up occasions, with full sleeves and trimming of cotton lace, such as were worn by church officials among the Spaniards. Deer dancers among the Tewa still wear these shirts. Finally shirts were made of commercial calico, with sleeves and collars in the modern style, but worn hanging loose over the trousers, as the old poncho hung over the breechcloth. The chorus at a Corn Dance is usually dressed in brilliant shirts put on in this way.

Moccasins — The Up-Turned Sole

Moccasins have a hard sole, formerly of buffalo hide, now of cowhide. In all pueblos, except Taos and Picuris, it is of the up-turned variety, mentioned in page 93. It is cut half an inch or so larger than the wearer's foot, moistened and turned up around the edges, so that it hardens in this position. Around the toe it must be crimped into shape. The upper is sewed to it with invisible stitches of sinew, which do not go all the way through the leather of either piece.

Uppers. The upper is of buckskin, dyed a brownish red, with mountain mahogany (Cerocarpus montanus) and sumac (Rhus trilobata). It reaches above the ankle and sometimes half way up the calf. It may be fastened by buckskin thongs passed through slits in the upper, or by silver buttons or dimes or quarters used as such, in the Navajo manner. Each man used to make his own moccasins though he may now trade for them with specialists. There are several different patterns. (See page 106).

Figure 1. In this case, the upper is all in one piece. The curved part, marked b, forms the toe and is sewed to the toe of the sole, which you

Man's embroidered shirt.

see indicated under it by dotted lines. The edge from b to a is then
sewed to the sole along the outer side and around the heel so that it
joins the toe piece at c. This leaves the projection c to d standing up
as a tongue. In the completed moccasin, the point marked d buttons
over on the outside. The upper is not sewed together but only to the
sole.

Figure 2. It can be cut much higher and the point e can be cut off as
in Figure 2, making a moccasin which comes half way up the calf or
more and buttons in a straight line, like a gaiter. Or it can be tied at
three or more points with leather thongs. (Worn by Cochiti, Santo
Domingo, Hopi)

Figure 3. Here the upper is in two pieces. The toe piece, A, is sewed
around the toe of the sole, B, so that the points a, b, c, come over a',
b', c'. The narrower, less regularly cut part of the toe piece stands loose
as a tongue. The large piece, C, is then sewed around the heel of the
sole, so that point d, on its shorter side, overlaps c' on the sole and e
overlaps a'. The point g then folds over on the outside of the foot,
where it may be buttoned, as Fig. 3 above, or tied as on page 107. (Worn
by Cochiti, Santo Domingo, Tewa)

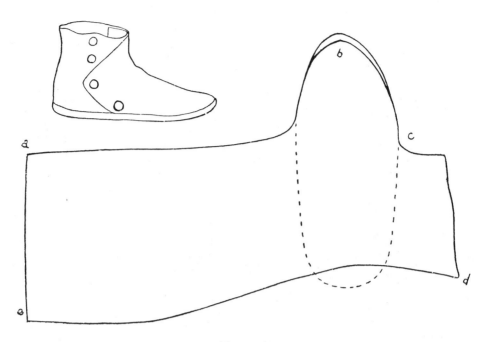

Figure 1
Moccasin with upper in one piece and button fastening often worn by Navajo.
Drawing by Velino Herrera, Zia.

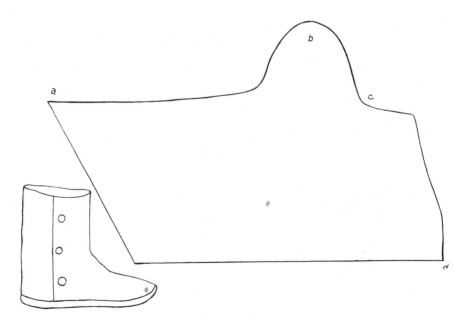

Figure 2
Similar to above but reaching farther up the ankle.
Often seen at the Santo Domingo and Cochiti Pueblos.
Drawing by Velino Herrera, Zia.

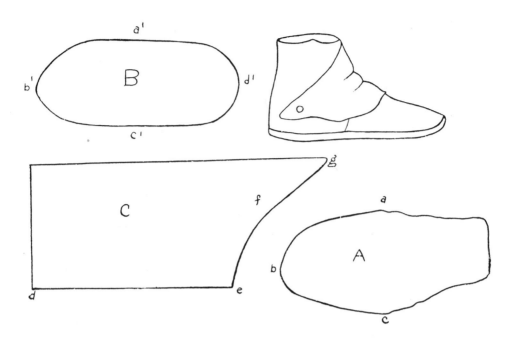

Figure 3
Moccasin with upper in two pieces.
Seen at the Cochiti, Santo Domingo, and the Tewa Pueblos.
Drawing by Velino Herrera, Zia.

In the drawing on page 107, a leather thong passes through slits in the upper and is tied in front. On page 93, the upper is fastened on the outside of the foot as shoes or gaiters are buttoned. There is an extra thong which passes through slits low in the upper at either side of the instep, passes under the foot, around the heel, and then back to tie over the instep. This is much like the way in which a sandal was tied and gives color to the idea that the pueblo moccasin was developed from a sandal.

The Hard Sole — page 108. This is the moccasin worn at Taos and Picuris, the pueblos nearest the Plains. It is the regular Plains moccasin, below ankle height and with a hard sole which is not turned up. The upper is one piece of buckskin, the length of the foot, rounded at one end and cut straight across the other. It is sewed to the sole so that point b comes over b' and a and c come together at the heel; ad and ac are then sewed together as the heel seam. After this, the slit d-e is cut, so that e comes at the bottom of the wearer's instep. Then the cross slit f-g is cut, just long enough to give the foot proper room. After this the tongue piece C is sewed in so that its points f' and g' fit under f and g on the upper. This will leave a little of the upper e-f and e-g, to be turned down as a cuff. Usually a drawstring is run around the ankle under the cuff from c, around the heel and back to g where it ties.

These moccasins are made plain for ordinary wear and, for ceremonies, they are beaded as Plains moccasins are.

Decorations. Moccasins used for ceremonial dancing are often colored turquoise or some other bright shade. They may have a band of skunk fur around the ankle or several very narrow strips of rawhide, wound with colored yarns, so that the strips, all together, make a pattern. Seen at a distance these anklets look like porcupine quillwork and, in fact, the Plains Indians wind rawhide strips with colored quills in just this same way.

Overshoes

In winter weather, Pueblo men sometimes wear overshoes made of undressed sheepskin, with the wool inside. Such overshoes may be an old custom, for Indians to the north of them make rough ones out of almost any kind of animal fur, to wear in the snow.

Leggings

Buckskin leggings of the sort used on the Plains were worn by some of the eastern pueblos and can still be seen at ceremonies. They were tubes of buckskin, reaching to the thigh, sewed up (with bone awl and thong) along the outside edge where a width of buckskin was left hanging out and fringed. They were held up by four buckskin thongs, attached to the wearer's belt, front and back.

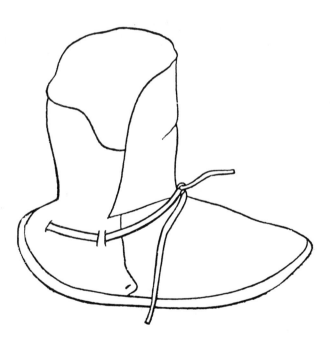

*Upper with seam across the instep, San Felipe Pueblo.
Drawing by Velino Herrera, Zia.*

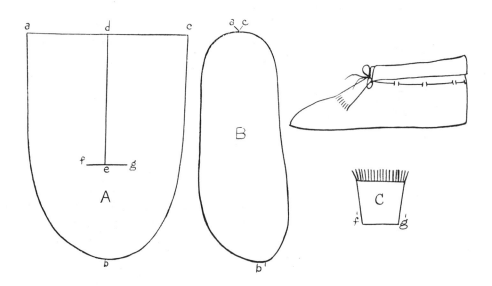

Moccasin with hard sole, Taos and Picuris Pueblos.
Drawing by Velino Herrera, Zia.

After the men had learned knitting from the Spanish they knitted leggings, or footless stockings, which reached from the calf to the ankle and were made very tight, to reduce the size of the calf. They were usually of black or blue wool, though the Hopi used white. Nambe and San Ildefonso made crocheted leggings of white cotton openwork.

Hairdressing

Pueblo men wore their hair long. For ceremonies and other religious duties, they let it flow loose as they do today. For everyday convenience, most of the villages doubled it up in a knot, at the back of the neck, as some Navajo and Pueblo men still do. Navajo do not cut the hair in front but Pueblo men clipped it in a neat bang across the forehead, with two longer locks hanging about to the chin at each side. Some of them speak of this as the "terrace" haircut. Taos men wore their hair in two braids like the Plains indians. They part the hair in the middle, draw the two braids forward and bind them, for a good part of their length with strips of some bright colored material. Yarn, in several shades, is often used today.

Ornament

It was the men who wore the most jewelry, not the women. They must have begun as soon as they had clothing, for some of the oldest relics found are beads, made of dried juniper berries. They began early to get something better than that. In the ruins of the great houses, abandoned before the Spanish arrived, are found strings of turquoise and turquoise ornaments, made by gluing bits of the stone to a foundation of shell or wood. They also like the shiny black jet which they dug up near the Hopi country and the white shell and red shell which other Indians brought from the Pacific coast. Dead bodies, in ancient caves, have been found loaded with necklaces of these materials which the pueblos speak of as "hard goods" or jewels. Short double strings of them were used as earrings which sometimes hung almost to the shoulders. Recently Pueblo people have bought silver jewelry from the Navajo. Zuni and finally, Hopi, now are making it themselves, with their own patterns.

WOMEN'S CLOTHING

Dress

There is no real difference between a woman's dress and a shawl, since both are simply oblong strips of material. In fact, the women often did change them about and wear any strip they had for either purpose. Today, however, there is only one strip which is worn as a dress and that is the woolen blanket, dyed in dark colors and called by the Spanish name for cloth, *manta*. The usual manta has two patterns woven into it, the main part being in diagonal weave with a wide border along each long edge in diamond, zigzag, or even plain weave. The main portion is generally black or dark brown and the borders dark blue. Some old Zuni dresses, however, are all black, and a few from both Zuni and Hopi are all brown. At Acoma and Laguna the women used to re-dye their blue bordered dresses in black to freshen them, so that the borders from these pueblos have a misty, blurred look.

In former days these dresses were left open down the right side, but now they are sewed up and sometimes there is a row of silver buttons down the seam. Along the lower edge, there is often a deep band of embroidery. Acoma and Laguna have the most elaborate patterns, in red,

Silver earrings.

blue, and green, with touches of yellow. Sometimes the Acoma men, who did the work, topped the geometrical design with a bird or two. Zuni embroidery is always dark blue, while the Tewa Pueblos, north of Santa Fe, have red and blue or red and green. No embroidered dresses have been seen from the other pueblos.

Belt

All belts today are of wool, though once they must have been cotton or even yucca or cedar fibre. They are much narrower than the men's sashes — only three to five inches wide, and are long enough to go twice around a woman's waist with the ends hanging down — that is five to seven feet. The colors are red and green, with a few strands of white, which shows up well against the dark wool dress. The patterns are a few standard geometrical ones. It might be interesting to note that the Aztec and other Indian women of Mexico tie up their wrap-around skirts with a red and green belt of the same sort, woven in the same way.

Plain Cotton Shawl

(Called by the Hopi a ''Wedding robe.'') Perhaps we should have begun our description with this white cotton shawl, which must come nearer to the first woman's dress than anything now worn. However it

Woman's woven belts.

White bridal shawl, braided ''rain'' sash and carrier, Hopi Pueblo.

is no longer made in dress size, but a good deal larger: that is, about five to six feet the long way and four to five feet the short way. A small Hopi girl, with the shawl wrapped around her so that the greatest width is across her shoulders, will be completely covered, with the edge of the shawl standing up around her head, so that she looks like a white cocoon.

The shawl is all of cotton, in basket weave. The color, when new, is creamy white and the weavers rub it with chalk to make it even whiter. Sometimes it is all of handspun cotton, though many weavers use commercial cotton string for the warp, which does not show. At the corners are tassels, larger ones at the bottom, smaller ones at the top, symbolizing rain and fertility. The relatives of a Hopi bridegroom weave such a shawl for the bride before she takes her new husband home with her and old accounts say the southern Tiwa once did the same. At present, no one but the Hopi even makes the garment. The bride makes two or three ceremonial appearances in it and then it is embroidered for use by the men of the family (Page 144).

Embroidered Shawls

Pueblos which had given up making these robes, used to trade for them, sometimes putting on the embroidery themselves, in their own style. Those who have seen the Zuni Shalako will remember that each of the tall figures is draped in four of these shawls, whose black embroidery, with touches of red, green and yellow, shows up strikingly against the white fabric and the turquoise mask (See page 98).

The same embroidery was put on smaller shawls, also of white cotton, in white basket weave. In fact, there is no real reason for speaking of these smaller garments as shawls rather than dresses except that seems the pueblo idea of them. Some people admit that they were occasionally worn as dresses, too. Then there were the dark woolen garments, embroidered in similar patterns, which were sometimes shawl, sometimes dress. However, old weavers say that they made some of them especially for use as shawls.

Bordered Shawl

(Often called the Maiden's Shawl.) This garment is a mixture, for it is a small blanket, of natural white cotton, such as the early women may have worn for a dress. But its border is of wool, in bright red and dark blue, the two imported colors. Usually, at present, it is a little too small for a dress and is worn around the shoulders by unmarried girls or by men taking the part of girls at ceremonies. Its size is about thirty-six by forty-four inches. The white cotton part is in diagonal weave. The colored edge, which goes along the two longer sides, has an outer band of blue, two to three inches wide, in diamond weave and an inner one of red, in diagonal. One old shawl has only red, which is bayeta, in broken lines. A few others have all blue or, occasionally, black (See page 96).

Moccasin

The woman's moccasin is made like the man's, with a hard sole turned up around the edge. Hers, however, is much more elaborate and so expensive that she seldom wears it except at ceremonies. It is of buckskin, kept gleaming white by rubbing with white clay and reaches to the knee. Below its stiff bulk the foot looks very small indeed and this is one of the reasons the women keep it.

Puttee Shape. Below appears the woman's moccasin worn in the majority of the pueblos. Here the upper is in two pieces, the larger of which is not shaped but wound around the leg like a puttee. The toe piece, A, is sewed to the upturned sole, B, so that points a, b, c come at a', b', c'. The rest of the toe piece, adc, stands up loose as a tongue. The upper, C, is a strip three or four feet long, made of half a buckskin. It is cut straight on one side but may be irregular on the other and grows slightly wider towards one end. Toward the narrow end, a niche is cut in it to fit around the heel and this is sewed on as shown by the dotted lines, so that point e overlaps a of the toe piece, already sewed to the sole, and point f overlaps c of the toe piece. This is all the sewing done. When the wearer puts the boot on, the loose point, g, is folded over the tongue, and the long strip, e-h, is wound round and round the leg toward the inside, finally tying at the knee with the long string, h-i.

Boot Shape. Below is shown the eastern moccasin as worn at Taos, Picuris, San Juan and Santa Clara. The upper is in one large piece, each upper using the better part of a whole buckskin. The upper is not sewed immediately to the sole but is sewed together so that it forms a complete stocking, the points f, g, a, b joining e, d, c, b, so that there is one continuous seam along the bottom of the foot and up the back of the leg with a good deal of gathering at the toe, b. The completed stocking is sewed to the up-turned sole, the worker first basting it at b, a and c, so that it will go on evenly. Here is another case which gives color to the idea that the pueblo moccasin was developed from a stocking and sandal.

The leg part of the upper is very long and wide. It is turned down at points d and g, which come just below the knee and then turned up

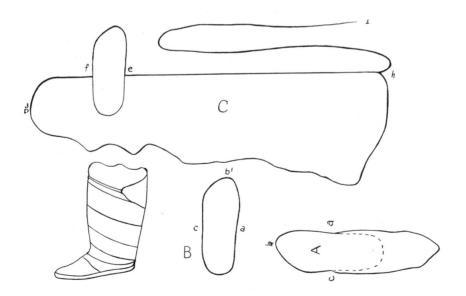

Woman's moccasin, puttee style. Drawing by Velino Herrera, Zia.

again, to make a wide fold. This serves the woman for a pocket. If her husband is a good shoemaker and has used specially large buckskins, he may tuck it into three or four folds. Such bulk around the calf of the leg gives the woman a clumsy walk but is considered very handsome. The large flopping boot is held up around the knee by a leather drawstring tied around the leg under the folds. It is kept from flapping around the ankle by another drawstring passed through slits in the buckskin, from the heel to the instep where it is tied.

Taos shoemakers say that the boot should always be made in this stocking form but sometimes the buckskin under the foot wears out and then it is cut away and the upper sewed directly to the sole. If the buckskin toe wears out, that too can be cut away and a new piece put in.

Hairdressing

Most Pueblo women cut their hair in the "terrace" style, like men, gather it at the back and tie it with a homespun string. Hopi girls, however, when old enough to marry, used to wear a special hair style. They had two disks of cornhusk, placed one at each side of the head with hair wound over them to form great flat pancakes. Or they might wind the hair over light frames of bent willow, so that it stood out from the head like butterfly's wings. When a girl married she gave up this butterfly hairdress and arranged her hair in two braids. This is no longer done today when the girls bob their hair (Page 143).

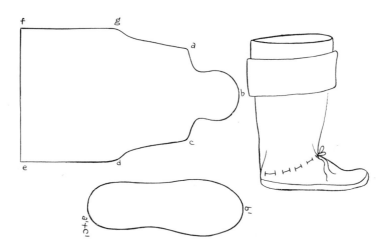

Woman's moccasin, boot style. Drawing by Velino Herrera, Zia.

Hair brush and supports for butterfly headdress, Hopi Pueblo.

Cosmetics

Pueblo people used paint and cosmetics. The moderns who buy these at a drugstore do not realize how much old-time Indians accomplished by grinding up minerals for paint, making perfumes and other "toilet goods" from wild herbs and using animal tallow as moderns use cold cream. It was the men who used the most paint, for, in ceremonies, it formed an important part of their costume. They smeared tallow on their faces and bodies and then put on patterns in black soot, red, yellow, or white clay, or dust of yellow sunflower petals. A man had a special little mortar in which he ground the paints for such a toilet. Women did not take so much part in ceremonies but they often put red spots on their cheeks made of crushed amaranth blossoms (Amaranthus hylridos pariculates). When sumac buds were fresh, they carried some in their clothing as perfume or they chewed the fragrant thistle blossoms and rubbed them over their skin. To prevent sunburns they rubbed on crushed mustard leaves (Erysimum sp.).

Men and women spent much time combing and washing their long black hair. Hairwashing, in fact, was partly a ceremony for it had to be done before any sacred occasion. Ordinarily each person did it for himself but if he was a performer in a ritual there might be some special relative who did him this service. The shampoo soap was the root of the yucca angustifolia, which the Spanish call *amole* from an old Aztec word, and the Anglos, soapweed. When the root is pounded, soaked in cold water and stirred, it makes a lather that looks like soapsuds and is equally cleansing. It was a blessing to people who had so little hot water, and the Spanish people soon learned to use it for washing hair and woolens. Many use it so still. San Ildefonso women had a hair tonic. They soaked Mor-

A Pueblo woman dresses her husband's hair. Drawing by Velino Herrera, Zia.

mon tea leaves and stems (Ephedra antisyphilitica) in water and washed their hair to make it grow. The brush and comb combined, was a bundle of fibers, tied together like a whiskbroom. Usually it was grama grass (Bovteloua gracilis, Tewa), or purple hair grass (Muhlenbergia pungens, Hopi). Sometimes the brush was a long switch with one end, where the finer fibers were, used for the hair and the other, with coarse fibres, for the floor and hearth. Hair brushing was a service which husbands and wives did for one another as a sign of affection. When young people were seen at it, it was like the announcement of an engagement.

LIFE IN THE VILLAGE

Hopi boys playing shinny

GAMES

An old pueblo was a hive of workers. On most days in the year, everyone was busy, from the smallest child, scaring crows or helping to bring firewood, to the oldest man, chipping arrow points or prayerfully getting ready for a ceremony. There was no regular day of rest. Yet, for days at a time, when there was no farm work to do, you might see people playing games. And not only children! Pueblo people are surprised at the white man's idea that games are for children and professional athletes. Pueblo games are for everybody, by order of the gods themselves.

Many of the games played now were invented and first played by the war gods, who liked to be gay and wanted their people to be gay too. But these games were not merely for amusement. Some of them, used at the right season, might bring rain or keep the sun moving. Others could foretell the future. The balls, the darts and the dice used in games were as pleasing to some of the great Beings as cornmeal or turquoise, and they were placed as offerings upon altars and painted on the robes of priests. This was not very different from the custom of the ancient Greek, who said that their Olympic games were invented by Heracles, a hero of legend and who inscribed the names of winners in the temple of Hera.

Of the outdoor games, the most popular was racing. This took place in spring and early summer when, said the Hopi, it started the streams racing down the gullies. Tiwa said it kept the sun on its course. There were two kinds of racing: one popular in the west, one in the east.

The Kick Race

The western kind was the kick race, where a runner ran barefoot, kicking a small stick or ball in front of him over a long cross-country course.

This game, said the Desert pueblos, was invented by the two gods of war, mischievous children who could change, at will, into mighty heroes. They never went anywhere without their kicksticks and there are charming stories of runaway children who found them in some lonesome place and played with them. Hopi, Zuni and Keres play it now. Tewa people say they once did but stopped because there are towns and railroads obstructing their old course.

And a kickstick course needed space. It was a circuit of twenty, thirty, or even forty miles, out of village, around some well-known landmarks and back again. For a big race, two teams would play, each with four or five good runners or any number that they settled between them. Each team had its "ball" which was usually a stick about four or five inches long. However, Hopi sometimes used a stone or a lump of hardened clay, and the Tewa a lump of hair mixed with pinon gum. The ball was started by one member of the team and then kicked by any of the others as they got to it. A good kick was about twenty yards. If the ball went into a hole, it might be lifted out into the open but if it were merely in a hollow or a bush, the player had to kick it as best he could. Men came home with their insteps sore and swollen.

The Hopi had kick races in the early spring saying that, later, the waters would race through the valleys rolling pellets of clay with them as the runners rolled their balls. Groups of men who all used the same kiva or ceremonial room raced against one another and before the race, they fasted from meat, grease and salt as priests did. The kiva chief, in kicking off the ball, sprinkled it with cornmeal, as holy things were sprinkled. In this ceremonial race, no one tried to win and there was no betting, but afterward, during the growing season, there were plenty of betting races, clan against clan and village against village. Young men practiced hard all the year to make themselves fit, and campers below the mesa would hear them before dawn, with jingling bells at their belts, running down the steep path to bathe in a certain spring.

Zuni people, too, began the summer with a racing ceremony, managed by the Priests of the Bow, representatives of the war gods. Afterwards the kickstick which they used was thrown into the river to be carried to the home of the Cloud Beings. Members of the kivas raced in this way, with all the people watching and the Bow Priests jogging along behind. Then members of the clans raced. After that, the season was open and any man who wanted to could get up a team and challenge some other team manager.

Still, the managers usually asked a Bow Priest to bless them. Men who wanted strength would not only practice but they would make offerings at a special runners' shrine and take medicine from one of the societies which specialized in speed magic. The active youths often raced without any formalities at all. They challenged the Navajo in the neighborhood, and Zuni at the end of the summer used to be full of silver belts and bracelets won in the betting. They even took on the United States soldiers, stationed at Fort Wingate before the Indian school was there. Zuni runners, they say, always won. Keres did not have such elaborate magic but they, too, thought of kick racing as belonging to the gods of war and they called it the "war captains' game." After the first race, they buried the kickstick in a cornfield, to make the crops grow.

Shinny

With the Tewa, the spring game was shinny. It was played with a curved piece of branch shaped something like a modern shinny stick and a ball made of deerskin. For the ceremonial game, the ball was stuffed with seeds. Like the "races," this game was not a real contest but a running with the ball, to make the waters run. Groups of men — one from each moiety — would run across the fields, driving the ball with their sticks though not toward any special goal. When the ball burst and scattered its seeds, that was a sign that the crops would be good. The Tewa and other Tanoan Pueblos also played this game for pleasure, stuffing the ball with deer hair instead of seeds (Pages 117 and 121).

The Relay Race

With the Tiwa, the great running game was the relay race. Anglos, used to seeing such a race run on a circular course, are puzzled when they see the straight race track at Taos or Picuris. It takes them some time to realize that runners start from both ends of the course and run back and forth until one side is a whole lap ahead of the other. This is the way it is done. Half of each racing team stands at each end of the track, with managers to choose the runners and start them off. Two men of opposite teams start at one end of the track and run to the other. There, they take their places behind the lines and the managers quickly start two other men back. So they keep running to and fro, but at last one side lags and its runners keep arriving later and later, until the other side is a whole lap ahead.

At Taos, on ceremonial occasions, the racers wear tufts of bird down to make them light and their running, say the Taos people, "keeps the sun moving.'' Isleta has a magnificent ceremonial relay race under the town chief and the war chief, with offerings, medicine water, and dancing.

Men were not the only runners or ball players, either. In old pueblo days, even the married women used to play, sometimes with other women, sometimes against men. Tanoan women played shinny by moiety, sometimes with the usual ball, stuffed with deer hair or wool, sometimes with two balls tied together. When they played with men, there was always a team of men against a team of women, usually married people against married people or girls against boys. That was one of the great occasions for tussling and courtship. Some of the Tiwa, in the spring would make a ball out of soft new leaves and keep it tossing in the air, men trying to get it away from women. If it fell to the ground, the side which dropped it lost. A more complicated game was played at Isleta, with a buckskin ball stuffed with feathers. A woman, standing behind a line drawn across the field, would bounce the ball out and then run to one of two bases for safety. A man tried to catch the ball before it bounced again, touch the woman with it and put her out. If he succeeded, she still had a chance to stay in the game by throwing the ball into one of fourteen holes in the ground. There is just a suggestion of baseball about this game and one wonders whether it is old or new.

Games With Sticks and Stones

Other outdoor games were played only for fun. There were special games for men, women and for children, contrived out of any bits of stone, horn or wood which could be picked up around the pueblo.

Throwing Games

One stone game was like the European's quoits or the throwing of horseshoes, so popular in country towns. For this a stone or corncob was placed upright on the ground, and the players threw flat stones at it, try-ing to knock it over. If it was not knocked over or if it fell with the quoit-stone beyond it, the player lost. If it was knocked over with the quoit-stone beside it, he had another chance and if the quoit-stone was in front of it, he won. Isletan women played at this game, putting necklaces on top of the corncob and if a quoit-stone knocked off the necklaces and fell beyond the cob, the thrower won. Mountain goat horns also made good marks to throw at. Boys held a sort of imitation rabbit hunt with these, for they would place a number of them on the ground, equal distances apart, then each boy in turn would start to run toward them, throwing his rabbit sticks as he did so. If he hit one, he could run again and he could take all the horns that he hit, as modern boys take marbles.

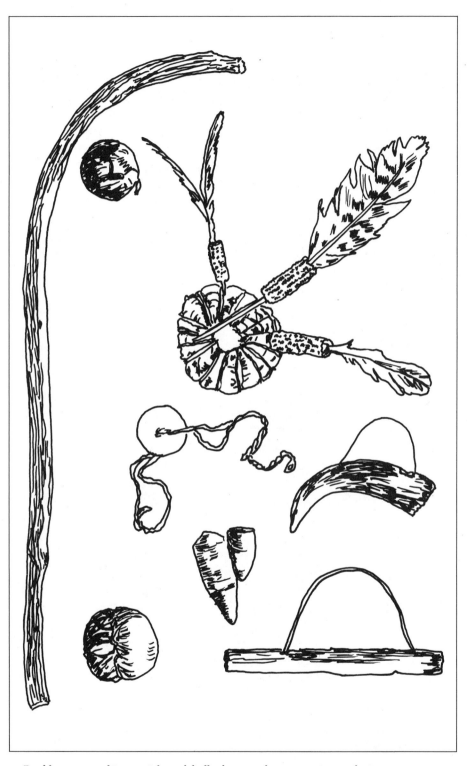

Pueblo games: shinny stick and ball, darts and targets, ring and pin game, tops.

Arrows

When the boys, or even men, had arrows, they played shooting games. They had excellent material for targets, for the soft cornhusks were exactly as good as the straw used by modern archers. Some Tiwa made a disk of cornhusk about eight inches wide, which they hung up. They would stand about twenty-five feet away from it and all shoot in turn. The one who hit it first, left his arrow there as a bull's eye for the others to shoot at. Whoever hit it, got the arrow. Or they might play by team and keep on until one team had got all the arrows away from the other.

Zuni boys made a stick-like bundle of cornhusks which they laid on the ground. Then all turned their backs while one threw dirt over it trying to leave deceptive lumps so no one could tell just where it was. The others shot into it by guesswork and the one whose arrow struck won the bets.

Sometimes the boys merely threw arrows, without bow or target. One boy held an arrow in his hand, like a pencil, and threw it along the ground about ten feet. Then all the others threw theirs at it, the aim being to have the feathers on the thrown arrow touch those of the arrow on the ground.

Darts

This brings us to the indoor games played in winter and many of these, too, have been taught by the war gods. One of their favorites had been that of throwing feathered darts at a mark. At Zuni, the mark was made of yucca fibre, wound up like a ball of string. The darts were slender sticks, pointed at one end and thrust down the center of a section of corncob so that their points stuck out a few inches from one end. The corncob served to weight the darts and had two hawk tail feathers attached to its other end to aid their flight. The ball was laid on the floor and the players threw at it from a short distance, the one who hit it the greatest number of times winning the game.

Another game to the war gods, used darts of unequal weight, some made of feathered sticks and some of feathered hollow reeds. There were three sticks and two reeds, all of the same size, then one reed of that size with a stick thrust through it to make it heavier and another large reed with a stick through it. The players sat down and threw only a short distance. The game was for the feathers of one dart to touch those of one already thrown and the players who achieved this took both.

Most of the above games were played ceremonially for rain, but also they were played for pleasure, with plenty of betting. However, the chief game of chance, played for rain bringing and gambling too, was dice throwing.

Dice

We usually think of dice as bone cubes. But such cubes are hard to make and the early Indians used many other things instead. Sometimes they had bits of bone, sometimes wild cherry or plum pits, but most often they used short sticks, painted in various ways to make them different. "Stick dice" of this sort were used by most Indians west of the Mississippi and down into Mexico.

Among these were the pueblos. Those in the desert had an ancient ceremonial game, with four dice which came straight from the war gods. These dice as they were made at Zuni, from sections of hollow reed, about six inches long and split lengthwise, so that each had a rounded side and a hollow side. They were marked as the gods themselves had marked them, two belonging to the elder god, two to the younger. Priests, or even gamblers who played this game thought of themselves as taking the positions of the two gods and each prayed for his own sticks to come uppermost. The players sat on the floor, around a hide or a blanket. Above them was hung a basket, upside down, with a deerhide or cloth tied across it. They threw the reeds up against this tight-stretched cloth, and let them fall on the hide beneath. The very method of throwing was a special one, taught by the gods, for each god laid the first of his own sticks across his palm as his "thrower" or "sender." Then he slipped the other three half cylinders one inside the other and laid them crosswise on the first. The scoring took account of how the "sender" fell in relation to the other sticks. In some games, it should fall on top of the others, in some, it must have a different side up. That is, if the sender fell hollow side up, the others should be rounded side up and vice versa.

This game, says tradition, was played by the Bow Priests to decide on peace or war or to foretell the outcome of a raid. They would agree, just as people in the Old World have often agreed, that the winning of one player should stand for yes and his defeat for no.

Wood Reeds

Wood reeds, another gambling game, used three or four hollow, unmarked reeds. The Zia have an ancient story of how one of their legendary heroes beat the town chief at it and won his house. People used to play all day or night and reach very high scores. They devised all sorts of methods for counting. Though the sticks were not marked with numbers, each could be given its own value and account could also be taken of whether they fell hollow or rounded side up. One Zuni method of counting was:

Player's "sender" on top	4 and another throw
Sender on top and all three others with hollow side up	10 and 2 more throws
All others with rounded side up	5, no more throws
Two hollow, one rounded	3, no more throws
Two rounded, one hollow	1, no more throws

If none of these happened, the player did not score at all but handed the dice to the next man. Score was kept with piles of twigs which players won from one another as modern players win poker chips. A more elaborate score could be kept by marking a circle on the ground and moving counters around it at the throw of the dice. For ceremonial games, the circle was drawn on buffalo hide and consisted of forty points, divided into sets of ten, with openings between them at the four points of the compass. The openings were called "gateways" or "rivers" and the counters which the players moved around were horses, pets or other animals. "Horses" were started at the different "rivers" and sometimes were moved in the same direction, sometimes in opposite ones. If the throw of the dice brought one "horse" directly on top of another, the lower one was "killed" and had to start over again. People who have played the game of *parchesi* will recognize the moving of counters at the throw of dice and even the "killing." They will wonder what must have been the history of this ancient game which came to Europe from India, but which may have been known in America before any Europeans arrived.

The game, whatever we call it, was popular throughout the Southwest and in parts of Mexico. It might be played with four dice or with three. The figures used might be round or square. It might be marked on buffalo hide, scratched on stone or put together out of doors by merely laying stones in a circle. This last was the favorite form of gambling. With it, the players used simple dice, made of split sticks, flat on one side (and sometimes painted), round on the other. Instead of being thrown up against a basket, the sticks were usually tapped on a flat stone and allowed to fall apart. A common way to score was:

2 flat sides up, one round up	1
1 flat, 2 round	3
3 flat	5
3 round	10

To give more difference between the dice, one of the round sides might be notched along the edge and then the scoring was:

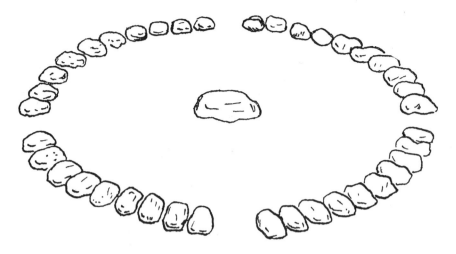

Circle of stones used for outdoor scoring in game of stick dice, (Mexican quince). Drawing by Velino Herrera, Zia.

1 flat, 2 round (not the notched round)	3
2 flat, 1 round (not notched)	1
3 flat	5
3 round	10
2 flat, 1 round (notched)	15

The Spanish people in the Southwest often called this game *quince* (pronounced keen-say) (fifteen) because of the highest count. We can see that any school group could make endless variations on it, perhaps enlarging the circle as Taos people did (to 160 points); or drawing some new figure as the ancient Hopi did, marking the route of the "horse" with circles and dashes placed around the edge of a flat stone.

Hidden Ball

Another well-loved game in all the pueblos and, in fact throughout the Southwest, was Hidden Ball. Here a bean or small pebble was concealed in one of four tubes by one of the teams. Generally this was done under a blanket for secrecy and, when the blanket was removed, the other team had to guess where the "ball" was. Hopi used rough stone cups for the hiding, Zuni had wooden ones, made by hollowing out the pith from one end of a section of quaking aspen. Most of the other pueblos used sections of cane. Often these were marked in special ways and each had a name. Any number of men might play but usually each side chose one to do the hiding and another for the guessing. After the ball was hidden and the blanket removed, the concealing side had to keep "poker faces" so that no expression of theirs should help the guessers as they pointed in play at the different tubes. To distract their opponents, the concealers usually kept up a loud singing and there were many sets of songs for this purpose.

The chief guesser pointed at the tubes and ordered them emptied out one by one. Usually the arrangement was that the third tube emptied should be the one with the ball. If this happened, the guessers did not score anything, but took the ball and had their chance to do the hiding. The scoring took place as forfeits for wrong guessers. At Zuni, if the ball was in the first tube, instead of the third, the guesser lost ten; if in the second, six; in the fourth, four. (Acoma made this last loss five.) The "chips" were generally straws and a game might go on for days, until one side had acquired them all. The bets had been piled up in pairs, shirt against shirt, arrow against arrow, and the winning side took the pile. This was one of the greatest gambling games of old days and there are many stories telling how men grew rich at it. Naturally people made efforts to get magic luck and at some pueblos offerings were made to the dead and to the war gods, while men would go out at night to the war god's shrine to listen for omens.

These are the best known games, but of course, they were not all played at all pueblos. And, of course, there were many variations and many new games, wherever people had a little time and some bits of reed or cornhusk, feathers and stone out of which to contrive amusement. The children, especially, played with anything at hand, imitating all games of the grown-ups and inventing others. A game the Hopi children liked was spinning tops. Their tops were roughly made of wood, but, instead of having a string wound around them, they were started spinning by hand and kept going with a whip made of a flexible stick.

TRAVEL AND TRADE

Life in the village was both pleasant and exciting. Pueblo people did not need to travel for amusement. Nor need they do it of necessity, since corn grew at their doors and they could get along very well with that and a few rabbits. They stayed at home much more than the hunting tribes like the Apache or even the Navajo. Still, they travelled now and then and often this was for trade.

Sometimes, for instance, a group of women would have some fine pots to spare, or an extra quantity of kaolin. Or their husbands might have jewelry, farm products, or woven goods. They would journey to another pueblo where they had heard there was a shortage of these things and, if it contained someone of their clan, they would go to his house. There they would be received like relatives, for all the pueblos which had clans used the same general list of names or they knew which were considered equivalent. Then anyone who had something to trade would come to look at their goods. If it was a fine day, they might sit out in the plaza, holding a miniature market. The sellers took whatever they could get that seemed of about the right value. However, a rough way of counting value grew up. All of the pueblos could use the square, dark blanket which formed the woman's dress and which was always about the same size. They came to count values in terms of this dress, even when they traded with the Spaniards, just as hunting Indians counted in terms of beaver skins.

Besides the home market, the pueblos had what might be called a large export trade among other Indians. Their corn, cornmeal, squash, turquoise and woven cotton garments were luxuries to the hunters and wanderers. Apache came to trade for them, bringing buckskin, moccasins, the baked core of the Century Plant and coil waterproof baskets. In fact, the pueblos bought so many of these last that early archeologists thought they must be a pueblo product and labeled them so in museums. The Navajo who acquired more horses from the Spanish than did Pueblo people, brought horses, sheep, skins and wood for fires and house beams. Paiute brought horses and strong bows. The Yuma and Mohave, who were traders themselves, brought parrot feathers from Mexico and shells from the Pacific. The Havasupai came from their remote canyon with baskets and a special kind of red paint.

Usually it was the wanderers who came, bringing their goods while Pueblo people stayed at home, secure in the knowledge that they had what all the others wanted. However, they sometimes made up trading expeditions, especially when they journeyed to the Plains for buffalo hunting. Then they would bring back dried meat, hide, and moccasins.

> Buffalo hides he shall find for me,
> *Costly things he shall find for me.

prayed the women of Hano, when their husbands set out. And the Tewa men sang:

> On the road to the north
> We go with our packs
> And there we will shout
> *And there we will sing.

This sort of trade must have been going on for a thousand years and more. Archeologists find signs of it in the very early burial sites. Burial sites of the Anasazi dating about 500 A.D. contain abalone shells which must have come from the Pacific Coast. In Mexico they contain turquoise which looks like the product of pueblo mines. The whole Southwest, as years went on, was criss-crossed with trails by which the ancient foot travellers went from the coast of the Pacific Ocean or the Gulf of California up the river valleys and across the mountain passes to what is now Arizona

*Songs of the Tewa by J.H. Spindler.

and New Mexico. They carried the ornaments which were most valued in those days—sea shells, macaw feathers and face paint, red or black. They brought back, principally, the painted pottery for which the pueblos became famous. Noting these signs of early trade is one of the most interesting tasks for archeologists in ancient ruins. Already they have found articles which the ancient travelling men must have carried on their backs for a thousand, twelve hundred or in one case, thirteen hundred miles.

No wonder, then, that there is so much likeness in costume and equipment throughout the Southwest! There is likeness even in stories and ceremonies. We can imagine a trading party crosslegged around the campfire after a day's slow bargaining. Beaded moccasins and silver-trimmed moccasins move together as the young men try out a few dance steps. Through the halting words of an interpreter, the older men go over the story of the two boys who visited the sun or the time when the men and women fought and separated. Each one repeats step or story in his own way and when he communicates it to the home people, it changes again. Of course, there were other methods of learning but the thousand-year-old custom of trade must have had great use as a news service.

WAR

The meetings were not always peaceful. The Apache, Comanche, Navajo, Paiute and Ute sometimes swooped down to steal pueblo corn, horses and women. Later, they took children and sold them as slaves in Mexico. Pueblo people had to defend themselves and the Hopi tell a gruesome story of how they invited a party of their Navajo enemies to a feast in the plaza. While the visitors ate, a Hopi woman stood behind each one, holding a heavy grinding stone in her hands. At a signal, all the grinding stones came down on the Navajo heads. The Zia tell of how nomads attacked the pueblo and how its men fought so fiercely that they could not be stopped, even when the enemy began to flee. The priests, who feared they would all be killed, sent out a young girl with a jar of sacred water, so that she might sprinkle them and bring peace.

Pueblo people say that they never fought except to repel these invaders. Yet, like some modern nations, they sometimes thought it wise to send out a punitive expedition and catch the enemy at home before he could do any harm. The Tewa had a song which made no pretense of liking such a task. They used to sing to their wives:

> For we are men.
> You have good luck
> For you are women.
> To Navajo camps we go
> *Ready for war. Goodbye.

---

*Songs of the Tewa by J.H. Spindler.

The weapons they carried were arrows, clubs and stone knives. Arrows, whether tipped with stone or iron, are not very deadly unless they are poisoned. Legend has it that the pueblos sometimes did poison their arrows by getting a rattlesnake to bite some meat, then rubbing the arrow tip in the venom. Spanish accounts say that the old Zuni Pueblo of Hawikuh kept rattlesnakes for this purpose. However, arrows could be used only from a distance, when the enemy were fleeing or when they could be aimed at from ambush. For close-in fighting, the pueblos used clubs which were simply a stick of hardwood about a foot and a half long with a knot in the end if possible. The scalping knife was a blade of chipped stone, from four to six inches long. Those who could get buffalo hide sometimes carried a small shield made from raw hide hardened over the campfire ashes and about a foot and a half in diameter. It was thick enough to protect a man's head from a club blow or from arrows, if he kept moving it about as he dodged. Usually it had magic signs on it which helped him with their power.

The war party painted their bodies. Tewa of Hano on one trip colored their legs white and chest and arms red. They wrapped buckskins around their loins instead of cotton skirts. They wore fur or buckskin caps on their heads and moccasins on their feet. The quiver and bow case was hung on the back, by a wide strap which went over the left shoulder and under the right arm. Club and knife hung from the belt. So did war medicine and a little bag of parched cornmeal. The leader, who was the war captain, or someone appointed by him, sometimes wore two straps which crossed on his chest.

There were usually some ceremonies before starting out. Hopi warriors spent three nights in ritual to make the enemy deaf, blind and stupid. At Zuni, the Bow Priests met in their ceremonial house and prayed:

> To be avenged,
> We have made up our minds.
> My children,
> You shall set your minds to be men.
> You shall think to provide yourselves with good weapons.
> Then perhaps we shall have the good fortune
> To get that we wish.
>
> Cleansing our hearts,
> *Cleansing our thoughts.

Songs of the Tewa by J.H. Spindler.

Perhaps other pueblos did something similar though many of the war methods have been forgotten now.

The aim of the war party was to hide near an enemy encampment and make a surprise attack when the people were asleep. If there were only women and children at home, so much the better! The idea, as in modern air raids, was to terrify the home population, so that they would keep the fighters from going out again. The attackers would rush on the sleeping settlement, set fire to a few tents or shelters and club the people as they came stumbling out. They took a few scalps, perhaps only those of the bravest, digging out with their stone knives a circular patch of skin, about three or four inches across, from the very top of the head. This was easy with enemies like the Comanche, who shaved their heads except for a patch down the center, but Navajo, Apache and Ute wore thick, long hair, which made scalping more difficult. If the party had killed a warrior, they sometimes took his deerskin breechcloth to cut up for bands which they wore across their chests. Then they made a quick get-away, before the enemy fighters could overtake them.

Half starving on their tiny rations of pinole, they hastened home through the strange hills and woods of the enemy country. They never went directly to the pueblo, but camped outside and sent a messenger. There was need for care, especially if this were one of the western pueblos and especially if the warriors were bringing a scalp. A scalp, thought Pueblo people, was almost as dangerous as the enemy himself. It was full of evil magic and if it were brought freely into the village, it would bring sickness and misfortune, just as the enemy would like to do.

So the scalp was cleansed and cared for until at last it was adopted into the tribe. After it had been washed, just as Pueblo people washed their own hair before a ceremony, it would become a friend. Its magic powers would be used to tell when the enemy was coming or to bring rain. The scalper too had to go through a ceremony, at least at Zuni and Hopi. Then he became a member of the warriors' society whose solemn duty was to guard the village against enemies, within and without.

So war meant ceremony, just as public health meant ceremony and care of the crops meant ceremony. The pueblos were religious settlements. Everything they did, in work, play, war and trade was under the protection of the Spirits. Often the dance or ceremony which accompanied some piece of work was as important as the work itself. We shall not describe this ceremonial part of pueblo life, which would require a book in itself. Moreover, Pueblo people prefer to do their own describing — or not to do it. To them, much of the power of a ceremony comes from its being secret and for them alone. They ask outsiders to leave it to them.

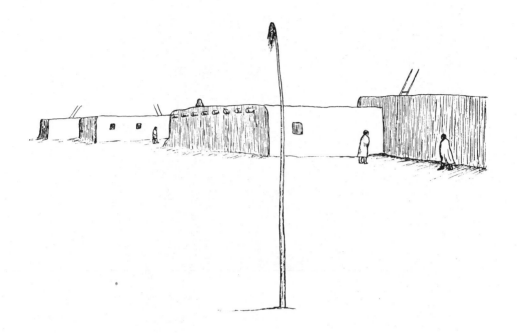

Enemy's scalp on a pole, Zuni Pueblo.
Drawing by Velino Herrera, Zia.

LIFE IN THE FAMILY

Indian family braiding corn, San Juan Pueblo

WHEN THE BABY CAME. There is an old belief quite unfounded in fact, that a woman who is going to have a child should not look at anything ugly or frightening. It would "mark" her child, thought the women of former days. Pueblo people felt, too, that the father of the coming baby should not kill or injure anything. So he did not beat his horse nor go hunting, even for rabbits, lest the baby be killed or injured at birth.

BIRTH

There were magical ways to make the birth easy, just as there have been all over the world, perhaps for thousands of years. One common way, which we can find described in old English ballads, was for the mother to unbraid her hair and untie all the knots in her clothing so that there should be nothing tight to make magic difficulties for the child coming into the world. Pueblo people had this very belief and many others, which, perhaps, we could match in one European country or another. They told the hopeful mother, for instance, never to start out of a door and then go back again; never to stop eating and then go on later, for this would make the baby hesitate in coming. There were, literally, dozens of things which she must do or not do, all meant to set an example to the child, so he would come easily and quickly.

When the great day came, the practical work of helping with the birth was done by other women. The equally important work of praying over the mother to keep harm away from her was done by the medicine man, but when there was a real complication, he used practical skill also.

The western pueblos, Hopi and Zuni, did not call in a medicine man unless something was wrong. A woman's own mother and sisters took care of her and generally, as we shall see, they lived in the same house with her in any case. At Zuni, they used the convenient arrangement of warming sand with hot stones and laying mother and child on this clean, soft bed which was easily changed. The baby was washed with warm water and then its body was lightly covered with ashes. "It keeps it from being hairy," say the Zuni, but there is a deeper reason for that. Ashes are used in many religious ceremonies to take away the effect of magical power and so they take away the strange magic from birth.

The eastern pueblos often called in a medicine man, even when all was going well. In some of these villages, especially the Keresan, the medicine societies or great guilds of doctors, were especially important and, as we shall see, they did the naming also. Sometimes there was one society which specialized in birth, as the Giant society did among the Keres. They had songs and prayers for good luck and also they knew how to massage a woman and to give herbs. In other villages, like Isleta, each society had one medicine man. Every pueblo, east and west, had some man whose magical skill could be called on at this dangerous time.

After the birth was over, there were ceremonies to take the danger away from both mother and child. The Hopi kept the two indoors, away from the sunlight for twenty days. The baby, of course, had been washed at birth and often afterwards. The mother, too, had a special bath every five days and was kept on a diet. The Isleta kept her in the house for twelve days and some other Tiwa for four. Even when she need not stay out of sight, she had a purifying bath which was not only practical but ceremonial.

Naming

The next great ceremony was the naming of the baby. The infant waited until its mother was ready to go out and meantime, with the Zuni and Keres, was guarded by a perfect ear of corn, laid on the ground beside him/her. Corn, the great food, was an augury of life and plenty. Finally the baby was ready to be taken out at dawn and presented to Father Sun.

There were plenty of small differences in the naming ceremony. The western pueblos, Hopi and Zuni, which counted descent through the mother, made a great point of bringing in the father's relatives at this time, as though to share responsibility with them. It was the father's mother and sisters who carried the baby into the light and bestowed a name they had chosen. The Hopi aunts and grandmother, in fact, gave a number of names, all belonging to their clan or large group of relatives. When the child was grown it could choose the name it preferred.

The eastern pueblos (Keresan and Tanoan) were those who usually called in a medicine man at birth and they gave him the task of naming also. Often he carried on quite a little ceremony in the house, making an altar of cornmeal and singing his sacred songs. Then he or, sometimes, his wife, took the baby out to the sun and spoke a name which the parents had given him or which he had thought of himself.

"Baby So-and-So is coming to its home," announced the Zia medicine man, as he came back to the house where the parents waited. They called back happily:

"Let it come!"

That first ceremony was only the beginning of naming. Pueblo people did not think of a name as a label which a person gets once and for all. To them it was more like a suit of clothes which had to be constantly renewed. A person has good clothes for special occasions and commoner ones for every day. So the Pueblo people first had sun names and then others which they received when they were initiated into any ceremonial group. Besides, they might have nicknames, according to their different activities, and these would change again and again. Also, they might have Spanish names, received from the priest and, if they went to the government school, the teachers might give them Anglo names. At home, probably, they would not be called by any names at all. Their relatives would say "My son," 'My sister," and others merely, "My friend."

CHILDHOOD

The First Year

The new baby spent the first three or four months on a cradle board. This was the regular arrangement for carrying a baby about safely and it consisted of a flat piece of wood, or of basketry, a little larger than the baby's body. The child was wrapped in soft buckskin or cloth and perhaps a padding of shredded cedar bark was put underneath. The child was strapped to the board with buckskin thongs and then even its little sister could carry it about without injury to its delicate spine.

The cradle board must be an old custom with the pueblos, for boards are found in the ruins. Yet once it was a novelty. We remember that, around 500 A.D., new people came into the country and that they had rounder shaped heads than the early inhabitants. These round heads were flattened at the back and many archeologists think this may have been from lying on a hard block of wood, placed like a pillow against the cradleboard. Perhaps this wooden pillow was a household invention which came in, during those changing times, along with the bow and arrow and the loom.

Each village had its favorite style of board. The Hopi, at least those of First and Third Mesa, made their cradle boards of wickerwork. Look at page 136 and you will see that a slender stick has been bent into hairpin shape, then a few others laid inside this hairpin, parallel to the long sides. Across them all, flexible sumac rods have been laced back and forth, in the same method that is used in a wicker basket. A little arch of wickerwork has been placed over the spot where the baby's head will be. All this was done by the baby's grandmother on the father's side, the old lady who is so very prominent in Hopi baby ceremonies.

The other pueblos, including Hopi Second Mesa, had boards of wood. Acoma thought that wood which had been struck by lightning was the best, for it had more power. Zuni liked to put a bit of turquoise inside the wood to give it a "heart." They cut a thin board the length of the baby's body, rounded it at the end and bored holes along the sides so that a cord could be laced through. The baby wrapped in a blanket was laid on the board and a yucca string or buckskin thong was laced across it, down through a hole in the board, up through the next hole and across the baby again. The eastern Keres and some of the Tewa now tie four ropes to the board and hang it from the ceiling like a swing. They do not remember whether they did this in the ancient times or not, but now the mother can move it to and fro much as a cradle is rocked. Swinging it thus, the Tewa mother sings:

There are many sleepy little birds
Sleepy little birds, sleepy little birds.
So go to sleep, my little girl . . .

Oh come, you sleepy little birds
And slumber on her hollow eyes,
That she may sleep the livelong day,
*That she may sleep the livelong night.

The baby remained on the board night and day except when it was bathed and changed. It made its legs and back grow straight, the mothers said, and it kept it from being picked up carelessly. As far as the doctors could see, the child grew up quite as strong as though it were allowed to kick. The baby was allowed to kick when it showed that it really wanted

*Songs of the Tewa by J.H. Spindler.

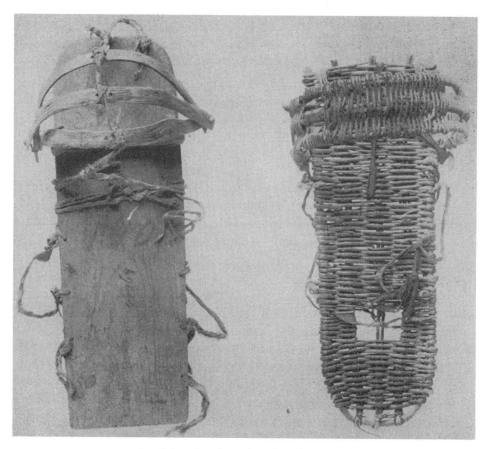

Cradleboards of wood and wicker work.

to. After three or four months the infant would be unstrapped for a little while every day when the mother could watch it. If it were a lively baby who yelled when strapped up again, it might soon be off the board most of the time except when it was asleep. A quiet baby might stay on the board much longer. But if the mother and sister needed to carry it some distance, she always put it on the board for ease of handling. At one year old, when it was time to learn to walk, it was through with the board for good.

Early Training

Let us picture a child's life as it would have been about 1880, the date of our story.

It is a summer day. When the first light comes through the little, glassless window, the grandfather makes ready to greet the day. If it is a Tewa Pueblo, perhaps he sings:

> Dawn youths are waiting for you to feed them
> *To bring you health and food.

Songs of the Tewa by J.H. Spindler.

Then he sends one of the children out to the door to sprinkle cornmeal or pollen to the Dawn People. Or perhaps he sprinkles it himself and says a prayer. The family have slept in their clothes, all but the very little children who do not wear any. Now they roll up the blankets and buffalo robes which have formed their mattresses and hang them on the "pole of soft goods." One of the women takes the brush of yucca fibres and brushes up the earthen floor where they have lain. The house is ready for the day.

Meanwhile the older boys have taken off their clothing, all but the breechcloth, and run to the river or spring to bathe. Even in winter they do this, breaking the ice for the purpose, for they have been taught that cold water will make them hardy. Those who are practicing running for some race or ceremony will run some miles across country as practice before they come back.

The older people and children do not go to bathe. They often take ceremonial baths in yucca suds and wash their shining black hair, but not on busy mornings. A little rinse in the water the women have brought from the spring is all they have time for. The long task of hair brushing, too, is left till later. They omit breakfast, for cooking on the open fire is a long task. Early Pueblo people were trained to work first and eat afterward.

The men start off for the fields, taking some bread left from yesterday as a lunch. They may have to go four or five miles and they will run most of the way so as to have time for a good day's work when they get there. The boys of eight years old and more go with them, to help gather up brush, or to scare crows. Our naked toddler is given a bit of bread and runs out to play with the other children. There they may splash in the rain pools or practice kicking lumps of clay as they have seen the young men do in racing. They may even try some of the steps of the ceremonial dances, with the pause on one foot and the complicated change in rhythm.

The women start getting the day's food ready. Two or three of the older girls are grinding corn. The mother calls to the toddler to bring some sticks of wood from the pile outside the door. She is going to bake or make some mush. The grandmother, and perhaps some other women, bring pottery materials to a place outdoors sheltered from the wind. The grandfather has gone off to prepare for a ceremony. Or perhaps he is a weaver who has his loom in the kiva or at one end of the family room and will spend the day working on a blanket.

They have a simple meal in the late morning, perhaps using cooked food from yesterday. By late afternoon, the work-day is over. The girls take the small end of the yucca brush and smooth each other's long hair.

Hopi toys.

Then they carry jars to the spring for water. That is when the young men, home from the fields, will be watching for them and even though they may not speak, each girl will know what boy is looking her over. The men come back from the fields, bringing some more sticks of firewood they have found on the way, and they too comb their hair. The pot of stew and the basket of bread are set out on the house floor and the family sits down in a circle for the big meal of the day. If neighbors come in, they are invited to sit down too. Before the meal is over, some scraps of food are thrown into the fire as an offering to the great Beings. They sit chatting, more neighbors come in and now perhaps the voice of the crier is heard over the housetops. He is telling about a rabbit hunt to take place in a few days.

"Work for yourselves for the next three days," he might say, "for on the fourth day the hunt chief wants you." Before he has finished calling the news to every side of the village, dark has come. The blankets and buffalo robes are again spread out on the floor and the family is ready to sleep.

It would be very different if this were the time of a ceremony. Then the women would have been grinding and cooking at high speed. The men would have been home from the fields, making prayer sticks or attending to their costumes, perhaps mending masks or borrowing jewelry. Some of them might have had to fast from meat, grease and salt or perhaps to spend the night in the kiva. There would have been announcements from the housetops every night telling what was being done. On the day before the feast, probably the whole household would wash their hair in yucca suds. Certainly those who were going to dance would do so. The house would be crowded with friends and relatives from other pueblos and it would be a wonder that the women ever got out in their best shawls and white boots to see the dance, because they would be cooking and serving all day.

It would be different, too, in winter. Then the family might not get up until long after sunrise. The men could sit about the house, mending tools or weaving. Or perhaps they would make a long trip after firewood which is getting scarcer and scarcer near the villages. Many important ceremonies go on in the kiva in winter and the whole family might be up all night, helping the sun to turn back; calling the snow or making other ceremonial preparations for the planting season. If not, since winter is storytelling time, there might be tales told in the different houses. Or the people might go early to sleep, getting strength for the next hard season.

The small child growing up would take as much part as it could in all the activities. The boy would follow his father to the field and copy the older man's actions. The girl would take the grinding stone and work beside her mother. There would be very little asking of questions but rather a copying of the older person's actions. It was an apprenticeship system, where the pupil learned by doing instead of being told about theory.

Nor was there much scolding. The child was told what was the right kind of thing to do and if it did not do it, the grandfather, father or uncle might give long talks about what was wrong and why. In the western pueblos, where the mother's family was so important, it was often the mother's brother who had this duty. Children were whipped, too, but only very rarely. There was not much sympathy for parents who punished too severely, for many an old story tells of a boy or girl who was whipped or struck, then left the pueblo, perhaps never to return.

Yet the children had something to fear if they did not behave. Anglo children used to be scared by tales of a "bogey man" who carried off bad little boys and girls. Pueblo people actually had such a bogey, or several, who visited the villages at least once a year, wearing horrible masks. One of them, called by the Zuni Su'ukyi, had a pack basket on her back, to carry the children off. The bogeys must have had some communication with the parents, for they accused each child of just the faults it had really committed. The parents pleaded for the child and promised it would do better, but if it did not, the frightful, wild-haired creatures, with their pack basket and knives, might come stamping through the plaza at any time.

If these bogeys took care of the bad children, there were other kindly beings who rewarded the good ones. These were the Cloud Beings or kachinas who brought the rain. In the western pueblos they danced in the plaza, magnificently dressed and often masked. In the eastern ones, where the Spaniards long ago had forced the most sacred ceremonies to be held in secret, kachinas came only to the kiva or to hidden retreats. They brought blessing to all the people and, with the Hopi at least, they sometimes brought special gifts to the children. A good Hopi boy would pray for a bow and arrow and the next time the row of kilted figures danced in the plaza, wearing their feathered masks of white and turquoise blue, one would step from the line and approach the excited child, silently holding out the gift. Little girls were rewarded with kachina dolls.

Initiation

When the children grew old enough, they learned more about these holy masked beings. In former days, this took place about the age of twelve or fourteen. Each pueblo had some religious organization to which every boy and sometimes every girl must belong. We shall not go into their varieties here, but note that this was the time when a child learned some of the religious secrets of his people. He was told never to tell them, partly because the ceremonies would lose their power if explained to strangers and partly, perhaps, because the Spaniards in old days had cruelly sup-

A ceremonial dance at Hopi.

pressed the Indian dances. The people had decided that the best way to guard them was to keep them secret.

In the next few years the young people worked hard, completing their education for manhood and womanhood. The boy did a man's work in the fields and sometimes his father turned over one plot for him to work by himself. If he lived in a sheep-raising pueblo, he might be sent out to camp with the flocks, or, in a village like Acoma he would take his turn at guarding the horses. He would learn to hunt from some older man chosen by his father, and perhaps begin to run down the deer alone. The girl would settle down to her three hours a day at corn grinding. The Hopi had a little ceremony when a girl reached maidenhood in which she ground for four days, behind a curtain and hidden from the sun just as women were hidden at childbirth. When it was over she had her hair arranged in the special "butterfly" whorls shown in the photograph on page 143.

This training was not coeducational. Boys worked with their fathers and uncles, girls with their mothers and aunts and the young people were not expected to be alone together. The same system prevailed in Europe a hundred years ago and many a Spanish or Italian girl scarcely spoke to a man until her parents arranged her marriage. Girls in those countries had their means of communication with the other sex just the same, and so had Pueblo girls. They would find boys waiting for them at the spring, when they went to fetch water. They would smile across the roofs as they stood watching a ceremony, girls in one place, boys in another.

But the great social occasion was the rabbit hunt. Out in the summer air, dressed in their best, the young people had their first good chance to run and joke and the old people expected it. The Hopi even had a special hunt for the girls "to limber their legs" after the days of corn grinding that brought them to maidenhood. When a boy had killed a rabbit, several girls would run to him and he would give it to the one first to reach him. That night, or next day, she would bring him a present of cooked food. That might be the beginning of a courtship.

In the western pueblos, where descent came through women, it was not at all improper for a girl to select a boy and make the advances. Many a Hopi and Zuni tale tells how girls came with presents of food to some handsome boy and when his mother asked their intentions, they calmly said "I have come to marry your son." In eastern pueblos, it was more often, the man who asked. The Keres say that when a suitor is rejected, he is "given the squash."

Whether it was a boy or girl who began negotiations, the parents' consent had been asked first. These young people were not going to live in a house of their own, independent of the old folks. They would be part of a large family, either at the girl's home or at the boy's, and that family wanted to know that the new bride or groom was a good worker. They were anxious about the future in-laws, too, for they would be exchanging gifts with them for as long as the young couple stayed married and they needed to be sure the new relatives would do their share. Then there were considerations of relationship. Of course the young people had known since childhood if they had clan brothers and sisters whom they must not marry. But the old people checked this over carefully and no matter how much flirtation had been going on, there was seldom a real courtship unless they approved.

Marriage

Among the ancient forms of wedding, the Hopi was the most elaborate. Here the girl led off with a gift of some special corn cakes to the boy. If he did not eat them, she was rejected. If accepted, she went to his house to grind corn for four days and show what she could do, while his male relatives prepared cotton and wove her wedding trousseau. There followed an interchange of gifts to and fro, each family "paying" the other, until at last the young couple was established in a room next to the bride's mother or married sister and a new working man was added to the family. Zuni brides brought their men home, too, but without the elaborate gift giving.

Isho, an unmarried girl with "butterfly" headress,
Mishongnovi Pueblo, Hopi Arizona.

Mogki a Hopi bride of Oraibi Pueblo in her shawl, carrying the reed container which holds other clothing woven by men of the bridegroom's family.

The eastern pueblos did not have such clear rules as to where the young couple were to live. With the Tewa and Tiwa, they usually made their home with the man's family or the young husband built a separate house of his own. With the Keres, things might be one way or the other. There were several kinds of wedding ceremony, too, though for many years now couples have been married by the Catholic priest. However, the glossy black, two-mouthed jar made at Santa Clara is still called a wedding jar and tradition is that the bride and groom drank out of it, both at once, as a symbol of unity. A like ceremony still takes place among the Navajo at a wedding, where the couple takes turns eating from a basket of special corn mush. In most pueblos, gifts are still given between the families of bride and groom. Spanish accounts say that once the Isletan groom's family supplied the bride's trousseau just as the Hopi do now and some Tiwa boys make the tall white moccasins for their fiancees.

The new couple settled down with older relatives all about them and usually with some in the same house. It was not the kind of starting off alone which a young Anglo couple expects. When the babies were born, there were aunts and uncles about the help train them. If one of the young couple died, these relatives were present to step into the breach. It was the same if the father and mother were divorced. Divorce was fairly frequent with the pueblos as it was with all Indian tribes, for people felt that if a couple could not get along, it was much better for them to part and try again with someone else. There was no divorce court and no alimony. In the western pueblos, where a man went to live with his wife's family, he simply picked up his clothes and went home to his mother. In the eastern pueblos, it was often the woman who left. The children stayed where they were and the older relatives who had been looking after them simply continued the good work. With such a large family, there could be no such thing as a broken home.

Old Age

Growing old meant more and more honor, for, in a pueblo, a man was not much thought of until he had proved his wisdom and industry over a period of years. When he had passed his active period, he would be in a position to teach others. He might have some ceremonial office. He might be on the town council. At least he would have his own grandchildren to instruct while their father was in the fields. The grandmother would be past the days of corn grinding and even of stooping over the fireplace to cook. She would help with the new babies and advise the younger women. If she lived in the western pueblos, she might be the female head of a family which owned important ceremonial property and the shrine would be kept at her house.

The Land of the Dead

Everyone hoped to live so long that they would fall asleep of old age. That was a frequent pueblo prayer. When at last it was granted, good and bad people alike made a four days' journey to the Land of the Dead. Certain great priests, it is true, might go to join the Cloud Beings and thence send rain to their people, but all others lived together, doing just the things they had done on earth. The only difference was that their winter was summer and their night day. They used the left hand and wore their clothes backward. A living girl who fastened her manta dress on the left shoulder instead of the right would scare her comrades, for that is the custom of the dead.

The departed ones needed food and clothing for this second life and so their relatives washed them, dressed them in their best and painted or powdered their faces. The Hopi put a mat of soft cotton over the face, to make the dead light in travelling. However, they did all these things quickly, for they felt that the dead person was longing to take someone with them to the other world and that those who stayed near the body too long might be dragged away. A relative carried the body out beyond the village, to some place where it was easy to dig a hole in the hard adobe, and often in former days the town refuse heap served this purpose.

The dead ones were placed sitting upright with their possessions beside them. Many have been found by archeologists sitting thus or lying on their sides, with knees drawn up. The pots with them have been "killed" by holes pierced in the bottom or by being broken so that no one else would use them. The Hopi sometimes placed a digging stick upright in the grave, as a ladder from the underworld, "spirit stick," it is called in English. Only children were not buried in this way, for they were too little to find the path to the other world. They were placed under the house floor and their souls entered into the new babies born to that home.

For four days after burial the dead one was thought to be lingering around the home. Every day the family brought food and water to the grave or they threw it out of the house in some special way. Even if they had only heard of the death far away, they did this, for otherwise the ghost might come seeking help. On the fourth day, the dead person was thought to have left and then the family purified themselves and removed all traces of the dead one so that the underworld would have no hold on them. Each pueblo had its own method of purification. Hopi washed their hair and the Zuni even took an emetic. Some Tewa washed house and clothes, and some Keres fumigated the dead person's property, while some Tiwa fumigated themselves with smoke. Then most of them did not speak, and tried not to think, of the dead person again. Thinking or dreaming of the dead only made one ill, so the living turned their minds back to their duties.

All but the widow or widower! At Zuni, these people had to mourn for a year or, some say, six months. After that they made special offerings to the dead and were ready to marry again. People tried to forget the dead as individuals, knowing that mourning and yearning is a sort of sickness which keeps one from being useful. But they thought of the ancestors all together, in their far away place, as a kindly force, helping to send the rain and clouds. Zuni people, in particular, gave them prayer offerings many times a year.

Little pine ceremony. Painting by Fred Kabotie.

THE PUEBLOS TODAY

North building of Taos Pueblo

THE DESCRIPTIONS IN THESE pages date from about 1880, the years when anthropologists first began to visit, photograph and study the pueblos. History has gone fast since then. Villages which could not be visited without driving over bumpy desert tracks for half a day, or several days, are now reached by smooth automobile roads. Many of them now have electric light. Many, at least in the Rio Grande valley, have water brought to hydrants in the streets. Outside the village stretch fields of wheat and alfalfa, far larger than the ancient fields of corn. In those fields you may often see tractors and threshers. There are wagons, spades and hoes to replace the ancient carrying basket and digging stick.

There are other changes than these, for the pueblos are growing and changing as they always have. The list on pp. 9-10 named 26 pueblos. Today we should add some dozen, farm settlements and sheep camps, which have grown up around the main pueblos, some a good many years ago, some quite recently. Generally they regard the main village as head-quarters and come back there for council meetings and ceremonies. Some of the "suburbs" of Laguna have their own local government, though subject to the main village. All this has happened because of new animals, new land or new government reservoirs and wells, making living possible in places which were too dry before.

Some of the old pueblos are being given up. Oraibi, oldest continuously inhabited town in the United States, is falling into decay. Its Hopi residents split into conservatives and liberals and the former moved out to Hotevilla, the latter to Bacabi and other points nearby. Many moved to New Oraibi at the foot of the mesa. Acoma, the high mesa which the Spaniards could not take, is proving too cramped for peaceful days. Almost all its citizens have houses down in the fields and some come back only for the chief ceremonies. Santa Ana, squeezed against the rocky bank of the Rio Grande, is almost a museum piece for its people to look at, from their new homes in the fields.

Old likenesses between pueblo groups are broken up. In these pages, we have spoken of Hopi and Zuni together as the Desert pueblos. Tewa, Tiwa and Towa and most of the Keres were River pueblos, with the two remaining Keres, Acoma and Laguna, in between. That was how geography worked out in the old days, when Hopi and Zuni stood remote in the desert, visiting back and forth and sharing customs while the pueblos of the fertile river valley seemed in another world. Acoma and Laguna, on the edge of the desert, were the go-betweens.

Now that is changed. Zuni is near the thriving town of Gallup, with its railroad and its highway, giving easy communication with the Rio Grande Pueblos. Hopi is still hard to reach, perched on its mesas, half a day's drive from the highway. In government administration, those two Desert pueblos have been separated. The Hopi have a reservation of their own (and it is a reservation, for they never received land from the Spanish government). There, they have an agency and superintendent, with high school, day schools, hospital, doctors and nurses of their own. The Hopi have organized under the Indian Reorganization Act of 1934, which permits them to elect officers, manage their local affairs, own land as a corporation and borrow money from the Government for farm improvements and advanced scholarships.

The eight New Mexico Pueblos north of Santa Fe are under the Northern Pueblos Agency and the ten Pueblos south of Santa Fe are under the Southern Pueblos Agency. Zuni, the most distant of them, has its own agency. Looking at a map of these pueblos and their holdings, you would see a variety of shadings which show how the land is held. All of these pueblos had land which was guaranteed to them by Spain, generally in the years just after their great revolution. That meant that it was not a reservation but the actual property of the village, to be used as its residents pleased except that it could not be sold or given away. After the United States had taken over the pueblos, in 1848, Congress guaranteed this right. These pueblos were to be among the few Indian groups in the country who had title to their land, instead of living on land owned by the United States and *reserved* for Indian use.

The Federal Government was careless, however, and Spanish and Anglo settlers moved into the fine green valley of the Rio Grande. They pushed the pueblos into smaller and smaller space. They used up their irrigation water. Finally, Congress ruled that the land must be given back. Sometimes the settlers' farms could be bought back. At other times, new land was bought, as was done for Zia and Santa Ana. Therefore, on a map of the pueblos in this jurisdiction, you will see one portion of land labelled Spanish Grant. Another may be called reservation, meaning that it was bought by the United States and handed over to the pueblo for use. Another may be *public domain*, which means government land open to all citizens, including Indians, for grazing and camping. Besides this you may see grazing permits, marking land hired for the use of Indian flocks and herds. Then there is land reserved to the Indians for sacred use, like the Blue Lake of Taos. There is even land bought by the Indians themselves, like the tract for which Taos once spent its funds. The land arrangement of the pueblos is among the most varied and unusual to be found among any Indians in the country.

Many Pueblo farmers raise crops for sale. Taos men keep cattle in their high upland pastures. Isleta has a fine herd, in the green fields beside the Rio Grande. Acoma, Laguna, and Zuni, in more desert country, are great sheep pueblos.

The older people in the market do not speak English but all the young ones do. There is a day school in every village with a high school at key points like Oraibi, Zuni, Taos and Isleta. Two big boarding schools at Albuquerque and Santa Fe furnish high school work and also special vocational training in farming and crafts. There are hospitals, too, at Albuquerque, Santa Fe, Taos, Zuni, and Keams Canyon.

In recent years the Pueblo Indians have received national recognition for their jewelry-making, pottery, weaving, and other crafts. Some of the Pueblo Indians have gone back to the pueblos learning the traditional crafts using methods and designs passed down orally from their ancestors. Other Pueblo Indians have combined the traditional methods and designs with new methods and designs that reflect and comment on the changing nature of their role in today's society. The high quality of their artwork is a mark of pride in their Native American culture and a determination to compete in the American marketplace without compromising on their integrity or the quality of their crafts. Though the pueblos are still tight-knit communities, every Pueblo Indian is faced with the difficult decision of drawing part of his livelihood and cultural roots from the pueblo and the rest from the world outside their pueblo. How much of their life resides outside the pueblo is decided individually and with the help of family.

The success and recognition they have received in the art world as well as their new political influence has united many of the pueblos, and helped them develop stronger pride in their Native American culture. The pueblos long ago decided upon a way of life and developed it to suit their needs. They may change the unimportant things, like clothing, transportation and crops, but the importance of pueblos as religious settlements remains central to their daily life.

PHOTO SOURCES AND CREDITS

Page ii: Frontise piece Fiesta de San Esteban, Acoma Pueblo. Photo by Frederick Maude. Courtesy of the Museum of New Mexico, neg. no. 103197.

Page 1: The great kiva at Pueblo Rinconada, Chaco Canyon, New Mexico after partial restoration in 1933. Courtesy of the Museum of New Mexico, neg. no. 48537.

Page 10: The eagle dance at Cochiti. Painting by Tonita Pena. From the 1954 edition of *Workaday Life of the Pueblos*. Original photo source: Laboratory of Anthropology of the Museum of New Mexico.

Page 11: The throwing stick as used by the ancient Basketmakers. From the 1954 edition of *Workaday Life of the Pueblos*. Original photo source: Southwest Museum, Los Angeles.

Page 12: Baskets of the ancient Basketmakers. From the 1954 edition of *Workaday Life of the Pueblos*. Original photo source: United States National Museum.

Page 13: Ruins of Pueblo Bonito at Chaco Canyon, New Mexico. Photo by Harold D. Walker, 1954. Courtesy of the Museum of New Mexico, neg. no. 128725.

Page 14: Ancient pueblo pots. From the 1954 edition of *Workaday Life of the Pueblos*.

Page 15: Ruins of Cliff Palace at Mesa Verde, Colorado. Photo by Jesse L. Nusbaum, 1907. Courtesy of the Museum of New Mexico, neg. no. 60649.

Page 16: Kiva at Ceremonial Cave, Bandelier National Monument, New Mexico. Photo by Wyatt Davis, ca. 1940. Courtesy of the Museum of New Mexico, neg. no. 6105.

Page 19: Coronado Mural(center panel). Painting by Gerald Cassidy, oil. Courtesy of the Museum of New Mexico, neg. no. 20206.

Page 20: Pueblo weaver with waist loom and Spanish style heddle. From the 1954 edition of *Workaday Life of the Pueblos*. Original photo source: Bureau of American Ethnology.

Page 22: Ancient Basketmakers' coiled tray. From the 1954 edition of *Workaday Life of the Pueblos*. Original photo source:United States National Museum.

Page 24: Woman shelling corn, Hopi Pueblo, Arizona, ca. 1900. Courtesy of the Museum of New Mexico, neg. no. 2571.

Page 26: Corn drying on roof tops at San Juan Pueblo, New Mexico. Photo by John K. Hillers, 1880. Courtesy of the Museum of New Mexico, neg. no. 40270.

Page 28: Ancient pueblo agricultural tools, Hopi Pueblo. From the 1954 edition of *Workaday Life of the Pueblos*. Original photo source: United States National Museum.

Page 29: A Hopi garden, receiving water seepage from the cliffs. From the 1954 edition of *Workaday Life of the Pueblos*. Original photo source: Soil Conservation Service.

Page 30: Hopi "waffle gardens." From the 1954 edition of *Workaday Life of the Pueblos*. Original photo source: Soil Conservation Service.

Page 36: Jemez woman husking corn. From the 1954 edition of *Workaday Life of the Pueblos*. Original photo source: Soil Conservation Service.

Page 38: Jemez women cutting wheat with a sickle. From the 1954 edition of *Workaday Life of the Pueblos*. Original photo source:Soil Conservation Service.

Page 39: Threshing wheat with horses, Taos Pueblo. Photo by Edward S. Curtis, ca. 1904. Courtesy of the Museum of New Mexico, neg. no. 143708.

Page 40: Washing the threshed wheat, Jemez Pueblo. From the 1954 edition of *Workaday Life of the Pueblos*. Original photo source: Soil Conservation Service.

Page 42: An oven for wafer bread, Hopi Pueblo. From the 1954 edition of *Workaday Life of the Pueblos*. Original photo source: Bureau of American Ethnology.

Page 44: Delovina Pino baking bread in the beehive oven, San Ildefonso Pueblo. Photo courtesy of the Museum of New Mexico, neg. no. 3712.

Page 45: Drying peppers and melons, Jemez Pueblo. From the original edition of *Workaday Life of the Pueblos*. Original photo source: Soil Conservation Service.

Page 57: Hopi peach basket in wicker weave. From the 1954 edition of *Workaday Life of the Pueblos*. Original photo source: United States National Museum.

Page 58: A Zuni fetish representing the mountain lion. From the 1954 edition of *Workaday Life of the Pueblos*. Original source: Bureau of American Ethnology.

Page 60: A buffalo dancer. Painting by Wopeen, San Ildefonso. From the original edition of *Workaday Life of the Pueblos*. Original source: Laboratory of Anthropology of the Museum of New Mexico.

Page 62: A Pueblo man throwing a rabbit stick. From George Wharton James, *New Mexico: The Land of Delight Makers (Boston: Page Company, 1920)*.

Page 63: Traps for small animals. From the 1954 edition of *Workaday Life of the Pueblos*. Original photo source:Bureau of Indian Affairs.

Page 69: Roofs, ladders and chimney pots in Zuni, ca. 1895. Photo courtesy of the Museum of New Mexico, neg. no. 5031.

Page 70: Making adobe bricks. From the 1954 edition of *Workaday Life of the Pueblos*. Original photo source: Soil Conservation Service.

Page 71: Pueblo women plastering an adobe house wall, 1936. Photo courtesy of the Museum of New Mexico, neg. no. 41589.

Page 76: Construction of a roof. From the 1954 edition of *Workaday Life of the Pueblos*. Original photo source: Bureau of American Ethnology.

Page 80: Gourds used as kitchen ware. From the 1954 edition of *Workaday Life of the Pueblos*. Original photo source:United States National Museum.

Page 82: Ancient pueblo pattern dishes. From the 1954 edition of *Workaday Life of the Pueblos*. Original photo source:United States National Museum.

Page 84: A Pueblo woman at her mealing bin. From the 1954 edition of *Workaday Life of the Pueblos*. Original photo source: Soil Conservation Service.

Page 85: Outline of a Hopi pit oven with vent. From the 1954 edition of *Workaday Life of the Pueblos*. Original photo source: United States National Museum.

Page 86: A Pueblo woman building a beehive oven. From the 1954 edition of *Workaday Life of the Pueblos*. Original photo source: Soil Conservation Service.

Page 87: "Buffalo Ceremony." Painting by Fred Kabotie. Collection of the Museum of Indian Arts and Culture/Laboratory of Anthropology of the Museum of New Mexico, cat. no. 24269/13. Blair Clark, photographer, 1991.

Page 89 (left): Ancient ceremonial dress. Painting by Velino Herrera, Zia.

Page 89 (right): Modern dress worn by singer at some ceremonies. Painting by Velino Herrera, Zia.

Page 94: Silver squash blossom necklace showing Spanish influence. Collection of the Museum of Indian Arts and Culture/Laboratory of Anthropology of the Museum of New Mexico, cat. no. 10.4/771. Blair Clark, photographer, 1991.

Page 95: Striped Hopi blanket. Collection of the Museum of Indian Arts and Culture/Laboratory of Anthropology of the Museum of New Mexico, neg. no. 70.2/644, cat. no. 9054/12. Blair Clark, photographer, 1991.

Page 96: Maiden's shawl of white cotton with border in red and blue wool. Collection of the Museum of Indian Arts and Culture/Laboratory of Anthropology of the Museum of New Mexico, cat. no. 45226/12. Blair Clark, photographer.

Page 98: Embroidered white cotton robe. Collection of the Museum of Indian Arts and Culture/Laboratory of Anthropology of the Museum of New Mexico, cat. no. 36416/12. Blair Clark, photographer, 1991.

Page 100: Man's embroidered dance kilt, Cochiti Pueblo. Courtesy of the Museum of New Mexico, neg. no. 73862. Photo by Arthur Taylor.

Page 101: Pueblo men's ceremonial sash. Photo courtesy of the Museum of New Mexico, neg. no. 815.

Page 102: Braided Hopi "rain" sash. Collection of the Museum of Indian Arts and Culture/Laboratory of Anthropology of the Museum of New Mexico, cat. no. 51648/12. Blair Clark, photographer, 1991.

Page 104: Man's embroidered shirt. Collection of School American Research/Laboratory of Anthropology of the Museum of New Mexico, neg. no. 70.1/1470.

Page 109: Silver earrings. From the 1954 edition of *Workaday Life of the Pueblos*. Original photo source: Laboratory of Anthropology of the Museum of New Mexico.

Page 110: Women's belts, Santo Domingo Pueblo. Museum of New Mexico, artifact no. 45156/12. neg. no. 72692. Photo by Arthur Taylor.

Page 111: White bridal shawl, braided "rain" sash, and carrier, Hopi Pueblo. Collection of the Museum of Indian Arts and Culture/Laboratory of Anthropology of the Museum of New Mexico, cat. no. 36414/12, 36799/12, 36800/12. Blair Clark, photographer, 1991.

Page 115: Hair brush and supports for butterfly headdress, Hopi Pueblo. From the 1954 edition of *Workaday Life of the Pueblos*.

Page 121: Pueblo games: shinny stick and ball, darts and targets, ring and pin game, tops. From the 1954 edition of *Workaday Life of the Pueblos*. Original photo source: United States National Museum.

Page 132: Indian family braiding corn, San Juan Pueblo. Photo by T. Harmon Parkhurst, ca. 1935. Courtesy of the Museum of New Mexico, neg. no. 4014.

Page 136: Cradleboards of wood and wicker work. From the 1954 edition of *Workaday Life of the Pueblos*. Original photo source: United States National Museum.

Page 138: Hopi toys. From the 1954 edition of *Workaday Life of the Pueblos*. Original photo source: United States National Museum.

Page 141: A ceremonial dance at Hopi, ca. 1895. Photo courtesy of the Museum of New Mexico, neg. no. 73438.

Page 143: Isho, an unmarried girl, with "butterfly" headdress, Mishongnovi Pueblo, Hopi, Arizona, 1901. Photo by Carl N. Werntz. Courtesy of the Museum of New Mexico, neg. no. 37538.

Page 144: Mogki, a Hopi bride of Oraibi Pueblo, in her shawl, carrying the reed container which holds other clothing woven by men of the bridegroom's family. Photo by Carl N. Werntz, 1901. Courtesy of the Museum of New Mexico, neg. no. 37544.

Page 147: Little pine ceremony. Painting by Fred Kabotie. Collection of the Museum of Indian Arts and Culture/Laboratory of Anthropology of the Museum of New Mexico, cat. no. 24266/13. Blair Clark, photographer, 1991.

Page 148: North building of Taos Pueblo. Photo by T. Harmon Parkhurst, ca. 1935. Courtesy of the Museum of New Mexico, neg. no. 4530.